D0339370

Stuck in Traffic

Stuck in Traffic

Coping with Peak-Hour Traffic Congestion

ANTHONY DOWNS

The Brookings Institution
Washington, D.C.

The Lincoln Institute of Land Policy
Cambridge, Massachusetts

Copyright © 1992 by

THE BROOKINGS INSTITUTION

1775 Massachusetts Avenue, N.W., Washington, D.C. 20036
and

THE LINCOLN INSTITUTE OF LAND POLICY

113 Brattle Street, Cambridge, Mass. 02138

All rights reserved

Library of Congress Cataloging-in-Publication Data

Downs, Anthony.
 Stuck in traffic : coping with peak-hour traffic congestion /
Anthony Downs.
  p.   cm.
 Includes bibliographical references and index.
 ISBN 0-8157-1924-8 (cloth : alk. paper)
 ISBN 0-8157-1923-X (alk. paper)
  1. Traffic congestion—United States. 2. Traffic flow—
United States. 3. Land use, Urban—United States.
I. Brookings Institution. II. Title.
 HE355.3.C64D69 1992
 388.4′13142′0973—dc20   92-12692
                                              CIP

9 8 7 6 5 4 3 2 1

The paper used in this publication meets the minimum
requirements of the American National Standard for Information Sciences—Permanence of Paper for Printed Library
Materials, ANSI Z39.48—1984.

The Brookings Institution

The Brookings Institution is an independent, nonprofit organization devoted to nonpartisan research, education, and publication in economics, government, foreign policy, and the social sciences generally. Its principal purposes are to aid in the development of sound public policies and to promote public understanding of issues of national importance. The Institution was founded on December 8, 1927, to merge the activities of the Institute for Government Research, founded in 1916, the Institute of Economics, founded in 1922, and the Robert Brookings Graduate School of Economics, founded in 1924.

The Institution maintains a position of neutrality on issues of public policy to safeguard the intellectual freedom of the staff. Interpretations or conclusions in Brookings publications should be understood to be solely those of the authors.

The Lincoln Institute of Land Policy

The Lincoln Institute of Land Policy is a nonprofit and tax-exempt school organized in 1974 with a specialized mission to study and teach about land policy, including land economics and land taxation. It is supported by the Lincoln Foundation, established in 1947 by John C. Lincoln, a Cleveland industrialist. Mr Lincoln drew inspiration from the ideas of Henry George, the nineteenth-century American political economist and philosopher.

Integrating the theory and practice of land policy—and understanding forces that influence it—is the major goal of the Lincoln Institute. The Institute brings together experts with different points of view and provides settings where they can study, reflect, exchange insights, and work toward consensus in creating more complete and systematic land policies. Through its courses and conferences, publications, and research activities, the Institute seeks to advance and disseminate knowledge of critical land policy issues. The Institute's objective is to have an impact on land policy—to make a difference today and to help policymakers plan for tomorrow.

Foreword

TRAFFIC CONGESTION has become a topic of everyday conversation in much of the United States because it imposes such frustrating daily inconveniences on millions of Americans. So almost everyone complains—but no one does anything effective about it. This book addresses both the causes of rush hour congestion and possible ways to reduce it. Unfortunately, reducing congestion will be difficult because its causes are rooted in behavior that most Americans dearly cherish—especially driving to and from work alone in private autos. Rush hour congestion cannot be reduced much unless many people are persuaded or pressured into abandoning that practice.

In this book, Anthony Downs analyzes the likely effects of adopting each of the anticongestion remedies that has been seriously proposed. They include raising gasoline taxes by more than a dollar a gallon, building more high-occupancy-vehicle lanes, better coordinating traffic lights on city arterials, and constructing new residential and commercial subdivisions at higher average population densities. Before showing how well each remedy would probably affect congestion, the author sets forth some little-known principles about how congestion actually occurs. These principles have vital implications concerning which remedies will be most effective. Building on "Downs's Law of Peak-Hour Expressway Congestion," first formulated in 1962, the author explains why creating more highway capacity usually cannot eliminate congestion, no matter how much capacity is added. In the final chapter he summarizes his findings concerning why congestion arises and what can be done to ameliorate it.

This study is the first in a series of books to be copublished by the Brookings Institution and the Lincoln Institute of Land Policy. Financial assistance was also provided by Peter B. Bedford of Bedford Properties, Inc., Thomas L. Lee of the Newhall Land and Farming Company, and Daniel Rose of the Daniel and Joanna S. Rose Fund, Inc. Their vital help is deeply appreciated.

viii   Foreword

The author also received valuable help from experts in this field who read and commented on earlier drafts. They were Kenneth A. Small, Clifford M. Winston, John Meyer, Herbert Mohring, Frederick Ducca, and Richard Tustian. Venka V. Macintyre edited the manuscript, Roshna M. Kapadia and Laura Kelly verified its factual statements, and Julia Petrakis prepared the index. Secretarial support at Brookings was provided by Elizabeth McKenny, Kathleen Elliott Yinug, Val Owens, Jacquelyn Sanks, Irene Coray, and Kathleen Bucholz.

The views expressed in this book are those of the author and should not be ascribed to the persons acknowledged, the funding agencies, or the trustees, officers, or staff members of either the Brookings Institution or the Lincoln Institute of Land Policy.

Bruce K. MacLaury, President
The Brookings Institution

May 1992
Washington, D.C.

Contents

Figures

Introduction

IN RECENT YEARS, residents in hundreds of U.S. suburbs have come to regard traffic congestion as their most serious environmental problem—and with good reason.[1] From 1975 to 1987 the fraction of peak-period miles traveled on interstate highways with volume-to-capacity ratios higher than 80 percent jumped from 42 to 63 percent; in just two years, from 1985 to 1987, the rush hour traffic classified as congested by the Department of Transportation rose from 61 to 63 percent; and throughout the 1980s, peak periods themselves became considerably longer.[2]

Unlike many other important American social problems—poverty, hunger, low-quality education, homelessness, drug addiction—traffic congestion is directly experienced every day by millions of American commuters of all income levels. They have become increasingly out-raged over the waste of their precious time and money caused by repeated traffic delays. Their anger has been the most powerful force leading more and more local government officials to adopt suburban growth management policies. However, myriad factors affect traffic flows; so the extent and intensity of congestion are still difficult to measure and track reliably. Therefore it is almost impossible to deter-mine scientifically just how well existing anticongestion policies are working.

Nevertheless, in most metropolitan areas, almost everyone believes traffic congestion is much worse than it was five or ten years ago. The statistics suggest that congestion is rising primarily in metropolitan areas that are either very large—those with a population of 2 million or more—or fast growing. According to the Texas Transportation Institute, the ten large metropolitan areas with the greatest congestion in 1988, in order of severity, were Los Angeles, San Francisco,

Washington, Chicago, Miami, Seattle, Houston, San Diego, Boston, and New York.[3]

An example of rising suburban congestion is found in New York. Long Island has experienced an immense increase in commuting since 1970 with little increase in road mileage. During the 1970s the number of commuters traveling from Nassau County into Suffolk County rose by 14,000 (or 70 percent). Moreover, the number *within* these counties climbed sharply: by 86,000 (38 percent) in Nassau and 138,200 (74 percent in Suffolk.[4] Montgomery County, Maryland, outside Washington, D.C., has reported similar increases: from 1978 to 1988, vehicle traffic on its three major highways increased from 58 to 83 percent while the population increased by 30 percent and the number of jobs by 45 percent.[5]

Why Reducing Traffic Congestion Is Important

From the viewpoint of people who experience it, traffic congestion is exasperating because of the time lost sitting in traffic jams and the frustration at crawling along instead of moving at normal driving speeds. From the viewpoint of society as a whole, traffic congestion is undesirable because it misallocates scarce resources and causes economic inefficiency. Formal estimates confirm that the cost of congestion is high. The Texas Transportation Institute estimated that, in just thirty-nine large urbanized areas of the United States, the cost of congestion in 1988 alone exceeded $34 billion, or $290 per resident. Time lost from delays (at $8.80 an hour) accounted for 65 percent of that amount.[6]

To complicate matters, government authorities tend to respond to public demands to do something about congestion by devoting more resources than is socially optimal to building roads and subsidizing public transportation. Congestion also causes urban development to spread more than it otherwise would because firms and workers try to reduce travel times by decentralizing jobs and housing. The total costs of these distortions cannot be even roughly estimated, but they are surely large.

Such distortions arise partly because individual drivers and businesses do not have to face the true social costs of their private decisions about where and when to travel or how to influence the travel of others. Consequently, the associated market price signals do not trigger socially efficient outcomes. For example, individual commuters do not have to pay the costs of the added congestion they impose on others when they drive onto a crowded expressway during peak hours. In addition, the commuter frustration that builds up in traffic undoubtedly helps increase interpersonal conflicts at work and at home.

The Focus of this Book

In view of the continuing concern about peak-hour traffic congestion, the time seems ripe to assess the public policies for attacking this problem. This book therefore provides an overview of recent research on the subject by transportation experts and land-use planners. It examines the advantages and disadvantages of the principal strategies being proposed to reduce traffic congestion.

The discussion focuses on three questions: Why has traffic congestion become worse? What remedies might reduce it? Which remedies would be most effective? To answer these questions, it is necessary to look at the effects of congestion on the allocation of scarce resources, the relationship between land use and traffic flows in rapidly growing areas, and the benefits of regional solutions over purely local ones. This last focus is particularly important because few local governments have yet recognized that traffic congestion is essentially a regional problem.

The Regional Nature of Traffic Congestion

The economic survival of every local community depends on its continuously importing and exporting goods, services, and workers. Hence all communities find it necessary to be physically linked to all other parts of a metropolitan area and the country. This occurs through an interlocking network of roads, streets, and other transportation arteries. Because of the regional nature of these networks, the traffic they carry is heavily influenced by conditions outside the boundaries of each community. Yet most communities fail to look beyond their own boundaries in responding to adverse local traffic conditions, partly because they have no legal authority over such external affairs. Their leaders seem to think they can control the factors that generate the traffic flows experienced by local residents. In fact, their control does not extend beyond the residential and workplace densities within these boundaries, the building of added streets and roads there, and local rates of growth. If most people who work there live somewhere else or the residents work outside the community, the local government may have little influence on even these factors.

A basic issue explored in this analysis, then, is whether peak-hour traffic congestion can be effectively reduced without a significant degree of regional planning and coordination of those factors that affect travel patterns. The required degree of regional control varies greatly among different anticongestion policies. However, for the policies potentially most effective, appropriate areawide coordination cannot be achieved solely through voluntary cooperation among the many fragmented local governments found in nearly every U.S. metropolitan area. Those governments will never voluntarily agree on how to make certain hard choices that affect congestion levels. Rather, each will seek to maximize its own residents' benefits and minimize their bearing of any social costs involved in cutting congestion. Hence the decisions necessary to reduce congestion effectively can only be made by one or more regional bodies with true authority and power not only over traffic flows but also over several other crucial elements. Those include highway and transit planning and construction, the location of key land uses, and at what densities new urban development occurs.

Yet any suggestion of true regional governance, even involving limited operating functions, raises many difficult questions: Who could exercise such powers, in view of the present fragmentation of sovereignty within each metropolitan area? Who could authorize such decisionmaking? What factors would regional authorities have to control to reduce traffic congestion? Would such control have to be centralized in a single organization, or could it be exercised by several, more specialized organizations? How could political support for such radical changes be found in spite of traditional American emphasis on local sovereignty over all land-use decisions? As the following chapters point out, greater attention must be given to these questions if authorities hope to avert the further increases in congestion that now seem inevitable, despite some more optimistic predictions.

Part 1
The Basic Situation

One

Causes of Recent Increases in Traffic Congestion

THE MAIN causes of peak-hour traffic congestion are deeply rooted in American desires and behavior patterns. Some are even built into the basic physical and social structures of U.S. metropolitan areas. Policymakers hoping to reduce congestion therefore must persuade millions of Americans to alter some of their most cherished social goals and comfortable personal conduct.

The causes of rising congestion can be divided into two basic categories: immediate and long term. At least four immediate causes have been identified, each of which tends to reinforce the impact of the others and thereby heighten congestion.

Rapid Population and Job Growth

Rapid growth in the number of households and jobs in an area inevitably increases the daily flow of traffic through it. Growth can be rapid because it is either absolutely large or occurs at a high rate or both. Absolutely large growth recently occurred concerning jobs, though not always population, in the twenty-one metropolitan areas with 1990 populations exceeding 2 million. All experienced substantial absolute gains in the number and use of vehicles during the 1980s, even if their total populations remained stationary. Absolutely large population growth—defined as a gain of 250,000 persons or more from 1980 to 1990—took place in thirteen of those large metropolitan areas and in eight others with populations less than 2 million. Rapid rates of population growth—defined as percentage gains more than four times greater than the 1980–90 average for all U.S. metropolitan areas—happened in eighteen metropolitan areas with population increases of 45 percent or more.

TABLE 1-1. *Growth of Selected Metropolitan Areas, 1980–90[a]*

Area[b]	Population (April 1, 1990)	Population change 1980–90	
		Number	Percent
Los Angeles-Long Beach	8,863,164	1,385,925	18.54
New York	8,546,846	271,885	3.29
Chicago	6,069,974	9,591	0.16
Philadelphia	4,856,881	140,322	2.98
Detroit	4,382,299	− 105,725	− 2.36
Washington, D.C.	3,923,574	672,653	20.69
Boston	3,783,817	120,929	3.30
Houston	3,301,937	567,320	20.75
Atlanta	2,833,511	695,375	32.52
Nassau-Suffolk, N.Y.	2,609,212	3,399	0.13
Riverside-San Bernardino	2,588,793	1,030,578	66.14
Dallas	2,553,362	595,932	30.44
San Diego	2,498,016	636,170	34.17
Minneapolis-St. Paul	2,464,124	326,991	15.30
St. Louis	2,444,099	67,131	2.82
Anaheim-Santa Ana	2,410,556	477,635	24.71
Baltimore	2,382,172	182,675	8.31
Phoenix	2,122,101	612,926	40.61
Oakland	2,082,914	321,204	18.23
Tampa-St. Petersburg-Clearwater	2,067,959	454,359	28.16
Pittsburgh	2,056,705	− 162,165	− 7.31
Seattle	1,972,961	365,343	22.73
Miami	1,937,094	311,585	19.17

These changes occurred in thirty-six American metropolitan areas, which were therefore most likely to have experienced rising traffic congestion in the past decade (table 1-1). Their combined population increase in the 1980s was 15.3 percent, in comparison with 9.8 percent for the United States as a whole. If one excludes New York, Pittsburgh, Nassau-Suffolk, Chicago, Detroit, Philadelphia, St. Louis, and Boston—included because of their large size but having low growth rates (or actual contractions)—the remaining twenty-eight grew 27.3 percent in the past decade. Yet all thirty-six combined contained only about 35 percent of the total U.S. population.[1]

Employment growth in the 1980s, which reached 14.4 percent, perhaps had an even greater impact in causing congestion than population growth. For every 1 percent increase in population, there was

TABLE 1-1. *Continued*

Area[b]	Population (April 1, 1990)	Population change 1980–90 Number	Population change 1980–90 Percent
Sacramento	1,481,102	381,288	34.67
Fort Worth-Arlington	1,332,053	358,915	36.88
Orlando	1,072,748	372,844	53.27
West Palm Beach-Boca Raton-Delray Beach	863,518	286,760	49.72
Austin	781,572	244,884	45.63
Las Vegas	741,459	278,372	60.11
Melbourne-Titusville-Palm Bay, Fla.	398,978	126,019	46.17
Manchester, N.H.	336,073	59,465	45.99
Fort Myers-Cape Coral	335,113	129,847	63.26
Fort Pierce, Fla.	251,071	99,875	66.06
Ocala, Fla.	194,833	72,345	59.06
Naples, Fla.	152,099	66,128	76.92
Bangor, Me.	146,601	62,682	74.69
Totals	86,839,291	11,521,462	15.30
Average	. . .	. . .	31.00

Sources: Bureau of the Census, *Statistical Abstract of the United States: 1991* (1991), pp. 29–31; and Joe Schwartz, "This World Is Flat," *American Demographics*, vol. 13 (April 1991), pp. 34–39.

a. Includes metropolitan areas with 1990 populations greater than 2 million, or those with growth of 45 percent or more from 1980 to 1990, or those with growth of 250,000 from 1980 to 1990.

b. Ranked by 1990 population.

a 1.53 percent increase in jobs outside the home. This meant that areas with relatively low rates of population growth nevertheless had more workers commuting daily. The Detroit metropolitan area, for instance, experienced an increase in employment between 1980 and 1990 despite a 2.4 percent decrease in population.[2]

Congestion is thus not growing at an alarming rate throughout the nation but primarily in areas experiencing rapid population or job growth. That is probably why the first congestion remedy tried by most local governments is to slow their own growth. Not only is rapid growth the most visible cause, but local officials believe—correctly—that they have more control over local growth than over any

TABLE 1-2. *Changes in Key Transportation Variables, 1975–90*
Millions unless otherwise specified

Variable	Increase	
	Number	Percent
Civilian population	34.0	15.9
Number of households	22.2	31.3
Civilian employment	32.1	37.4
Licensed drivers	38.0	29.3
Cars and light trucks in use	45.8	41.9
All cars and trucks in use	59.2	49.3
Total vehicle miles traveled annually		
All motor vehicles	821.8	61.9
All passenger cars	451.5	43.6
Annual miles traveled per vehicle[a]		
All motor vehicles	1,365	14.2
All passenger cars	692	7.1

Sources: Motor Vehicle Manufacturers Association, *Motor Vehicle Facts and Figures '91* (Detroit, 1991), pp. 28–29, 38–39, 43, 53; and Bureau of the Census, *Statistical Abstract of the United States: 1982–83*, pp. 7, 45, 384, 614.
a. For 1975–89.

other cause. Also, for reasons discussed later, they feel they are less likely to upset voters by adopting growth-slowing policies than by using other congestion remedies.

More Intensive Use of Automotive Vehicles

During the past fifteen years, the intensity with which Americans have used automotive vehicles has risen sharply. This has compounded the increase in vehicle travel resulting from population growth alone. Thus the number of cars and trucks in use increased nearly 50 percent, and the number of miles driven per vehicle increased 14.2 percent (table 1-2). Hence the total number of miles traveled by all motor vehicles annually soared 61.9 percent. The number of cars and light trucks available for personal driving during peak periods rose twice as fast as the number of households in absolute terms and one-third faster in relative terms. It also rose much faster than the number of licensed drivers. Total motor vehicle miles traveled increased faster than any other variable shown in table 1-2.

This intensified use of vehicles has contributed even more than population growth to the worsening congestion, except in very fast-growing areas. Consider a typical metropolitan area containing 100,000 residents in 1975. From 1975 to 1990 the number of vehicles in use would have risen 29.7 percent even if there had been no population growth at all. The number of miles driven per vehicle increased too; so total vehicle miles driven would have shot up 51.9 percent—also without any population rise. However, during the same fifteen years the nation's total population rose 15.2 percent. If this community had grown at that same rate, by 1990 its total population would be generating 75 percent more vehicle miles of driving than in 1975.[3]

The widespread occurrence of this vehicle population explosion is shown by table 1-3. From 1980 to 1990 the absolute number of registered vehicles rose 34.4 million, or 55.2 percent more than the human population, which grew by 22.2 million. Vehicle populations increased more than human populations in thirty-six states and the District of Columbia.

This intensification of vehicle ownership and usage can be traced in part to the sharp increase in households having more than one person working outside the home, as more women entered the job market. The fraction of all households owning two or more vehicles rose from 29 percent in 1969 to 53 percent in 1988.[4] Vehicle usage was also affected by the growth of suburbs not well served by public transit, the scattering of jobs, and a decline in the use of public transit for commuting trips.

Failure to Build New Roads

Between 1981 and 1989, total highway mileage in the United States went from 3.853 million to 3.877 million, an increase of only 0.6 percent in a period when the number of cars and trucks in use rose by 24.0 percent and total vehicle miles driven soared 33.6 percent.[5] Urban road mileage went from 624,000 miles in 1980 to 753,000 in 1989, a gain of 20.7 percent.[6] These data do not take into account the widening of existing roads. But the Texas Transportation Institute compared changes in daily vehicle miles traveled with changes in lane miles of both expressways and major arteries in thirty-nine large urban areas for 1982–88. Total driving increased more than twice as fast as roadway

TABLE 1-3. *Changes in Population and Number of Automotive Vehicles, by State, 1980–90*

State	Change in population		Change in registered automotive vehicles		Ratio of change in vehicle numbers to change in population	Vehicles per 100 persons 1990
	Thousands	Percent	Thousands	Percent		
Alabama	150	3.9	745	25.36	4.97	91.2
Alaska	150	37.5	106	40.46	0.71	66.9
Arizona	947	34.8	934	48.72	0.99	77.8
Arkansas	64	2.8	−126	−8.01	−1.97	61.6
California	6,091	25.7	5,303	31.43	0.87	74.5
Colorado	405	14.0	902	38.51	2.23	98.5
Connecticut	179	5.8	525	24.45	2.93	81.3
Delaware	71	11.9	134	33.75	1.89	79.7
District of Columbia	−32	−5.0	−14	−5.22	0.44	41.9
Florida	3,197	32.8	3,918	51.46	1.23	89.1
Georgia	1,014	18.6	1,560	40.86	1.54	83.0
Hawaii	143	14.8	190	33.33	1.33	68.6
Idaho	62	6.6	200	23.98	3.23	102.7
Illinois	12	0.1	646	8.64	53.83	71.1
Indiana	54	1.0	588	15.37	10.89	79.6
Iowa	−137	−4.7	270	11.59	−1.97	93.6
Kansas	114	4.8	−5	−0.25	−0.04	80.8
Kentucky	24	0.7	297	11.45	12.38	78.4
Louisiana	15	0.4	234	8.42	15.60	71.4
Maine	102	9.1	222	30.66	2.18	77.0
Maryland	565	13.4	777	27.72	1.38	74.9
Massachusetts	279	4.9	38	1.01	0.14	62.9
Michigan	37	0.4	722	11.13	19.51	77.6
Minnesota	298	7.3	250	8.09	0.84	76.4
Mississippi	52	2.1	325	20.61	6.25	73.9

capacity. As a result, the number of urban areas classified by the institute as suffering from congestion rose from ten in 1982 to eighteen in 1988. Thirty-five of the thirty-nine areas had higher congestion indexes in 1988 than in 1982.[7]

Failure to Make Drivers Bear Full Costs They Generate

Another immediate cause of traffic congestion long noted by economists but ignored by government officials is that commuters are not

TABLE 1-3. *Continued*

State	Change in population		Change in registered automotive vehicles		Ratio of change in vehicle numbers to change in population	Vehicles per 100 persons 1990
	Thousands	Percent	Thousands	Percent		
Missouri	200	4.1	619	18.92	3.10	76.0
Montana	12	1.5	78	11.47	6.50	94.9
Nebraska	8	0.5	133	10.61	16.63	87.9
Nevada	402	50.3	192	29.31	0.48	70.5
New Hampshire	188	20.4	251	35.65	1.34	86.1
New Jersey	366	5.0	832	17.48	2.27	72.4
New Mexico	215	16.5	251	23.50	1.17	87.1
New York	432	2.5	2,155	26.93	4.99	56.5
North Carolina	754	12.8	694	15.31	0.92	78.8
North Dakota	−15	−2.3	2	0.32	−0.13	98.5
Ohio	50	0.5	1,620	20.85	32.40	86.6
Oklahoma	120	4.0	9	0.35	0.08	82.4
Oregon	209	7.9	359	17.25	1.72	85.8
Pennsylvania	14	0.1	1,101	15.90	78.64	67.6
Rhode Island	56	5.9	46	7.38	0.82	66.7
South Carolina	367	11.8	559	28.01	1.52	73.3
South Dakota	6	0.9	121	20.13	20.17	103.7
Tennessee	286	6.2	1,138	34.79	3.98	90.4
Texas	2,758	19.4	2,233	21.32	0.81	74.8
Utah	261	17.9	199	20.06	0.76	69.1
Vermont	51	10.0	123	35.45	2.41	83.5
Virginia	841	15.7	1,356	37.40	1.61	80.5
Washington	736	17.8	1,066	33.05	1.45	88.2
West Virginia	−157	−8.1	−98	−7.42	0.62	68.1
Wisconsin	186	4.0	626	21.29	3.37	72.9
Wyoming	−18	−3.8	26	5.57	−1.44	108.7
United States	22,184	9.8	34,432	22.10	1.55	76.5

Sources: Human populations data are from *Numbers News*, vol. 11 (February 1991), p. 2. Vehicle populations data are from Bureau of the Census, *Statistical Abstract of the United States, 1982–83*, p. 614; Motor Vehicle Manufacturers Association, *Motor Vehicle Facts and Figures '91* (Detroit, 1991), p. 22.

required to pay the full marginal costs of driving during peak periods. Drivers are only responsible for vehicle operating costs and the time spent commuting. Since they will probably be caught in heavy congestion during peak periods, they recognize that their commuting time will be higher then than during other periods. But by commuting during peak hours, each employee can work the same hours as most others do. As long as this benefit outweighs the private costs described earlier, many commuters will travel in peak periods.

What these drivers fail to consider, however, are the costs of delay that their entry imposes on all other persons traveling along a congested roadway at the same time. Unless society compels them to do otherwise—say, by charging a toll or parking fee for driving during the most popular periods, as explained in chapters 4 and 5—commuters will continue to underestimate this collective cost. The main reason they and most public officials think this way is that traditionally most roads have been freely accessible to all motorists. People could certainly recognize that offering unlimited access to hearty free meals at restaurants would cause chronic overcrowding there, as happens at many shelters for the homeless. Similarly, they see that offering public housing units at below cost has generated massive waiting lists among potential occupants. But they fail to connect the congestion they abhor with free access to crowded expressways during peak hours. Clearly, no strategy for remedying peak-hour congestion will be effective unless this relationship is fully recognized and taken into account.

Long-Term Causes

Suburban traffic congestion in growing metropolitan areas is also intensified by a number of long-term, or indirect, causes.

Concentration of Work Trips in Time

Many work trips are concentrated in relatively short periods each day, mainly in the morning (6 to 9 a.m.) and evening (4 to 7 p.m.) rush hours. About 17 percent of all trips occur during the morning peak period, and 23 percent during the evening peak (figure 1-1). The heaviest concentration per hour is from 4 to 7 p.m. for all trips, and from 6 to 9 a.m. for work trips. Since 1983 this concentration has been compounded by a 25.2 percent increase in the total number of vehicle

FIGURE 1-1. *Share of Weekday Vehicle Trip Miles, by Type of Trip and Time Period*

Percent

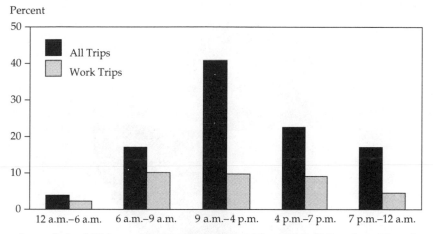

Source: Federal Highway Administration, *Personal Travel in the U.S.*, vol. 1: *1983–1984 Nationwide Personal Transportation Study* (Department of Transportation, 1986).

trips made daily and by a 40.6 percent jump in the total vehicle miles driven daily.[8]

Trips cluster in this way because most organizations start and end their work days at the same time so that their employees can interact with workers in other organizations. The resulting efficiency is thought to outweigh the costs of delay that arise because their workers all have to commute at the same time.[9] As long as organizations hold this view, they will continue to have roughly the same working hours.

Currently, the private marginal costs of the work pattern for each firm are smaller than the social marginal costs it causes. Each firm suffers—mainly indirectly—only from the time losses its own employees experience commuting to work; it does not have to pay any of the costs their peak-hour travel imposes on other firms and workers. Firms thus put less effort into adjusting work hours than they would if they had to pay the full costs of the present arrangement. This causes a socially inefficient allocation of resources. It could be corrected by placing a price on travel during peak hours through assessing special tolls (see chapter 4).

Many nonwork trips are also concentrated close to the peak commuting periods: people taking children to school or running errands before or after work. In 1983 weekday nonwork trips made up 49.7

FIGURE 1-2. *Distribution of Average Commuting Times in U.S. Metropolitan Areas, 1980*

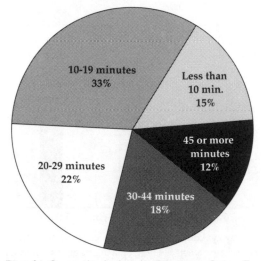

Source: Alan E. Pisarski, *Commuting in America* (Westport, Conn.: Eno Foundation for Transportation, 1987), p. 60.

percent of all morning peak-hour trips and 68.9 percent of all evening peak-hour trips.[10]

Desire to Choose Where to Live and Work

Many commuters are willing to travel long distances or to tolerate the time wasted in heavy traffic so they can work and live where they choose. If they commute relatively long distances, they add to total peak-period travel. In 1980 the average commuting trip took 21.7 minutes, but 30 percent of all commuters traveled 30 minutes or more, and 12 percent traveled 45 minutes or more (figure 1-2). In large metropolitan areas the average trip time is longer and the percentage of commuters traveling for long periods is higher. In the New York City area, for example, the average commuting time was 32.3 minutes, and nearly 30 percent of all commuters traveled 45 minutes or more.[11]

From 1983 to 1990 the average work trip has increased from 8.6 miles to 10.98 miles (or 27 percent).[12] People's willingness to commute long distances has repeatedly undermined attempts to shorten commuting times by building housing near workplaces and encouraging workers to occupy that housing (see chapter 7). Almost invariably, many choose to live in distant communities, while many occupants of the adjacent housing work miles away.

The reasons for this behavior are rooted in fundamental American values. In a 1980 national sample of workers commuting more than five miles to and from work daily, respondents were asked to state the most important reason they lived so far from their jobs. About 38 percent cited good schools; 24 percent said they liked their house; 17 percent said they liked their neighbors; and 10 percent said their own jobs were too far from the jobs of other family members.[13]

Desire for Low-Density Neighborhoods

A goal of most American households is to own single-family detached homes with private open space next to each dwelling. The low-density pattern required to meet this goal spreads housing over a much larger area than it would occupy in high-density settlements. Thus it is not surprising that central cities' share of all metropolitan-area workers' homes declined from 53.2 to 45.7 percent in the 1970s.[14]

The nation's average residential densities have also been affected by the relative movement of population from metropolitan areas in the Northeast and Midwest to ones in the South and West built mainly in the automobile era. Of the 182 cities that contained more than 100,000 persons in 1986, the 22 in the Northeast had an average density more than triple that of the 39 in the Midwest and more than six times the average of cities in the other three regions (table 1-4).

Density in the suburbs—computed for seven metropolitan areas in the Northeast and Midwest (total population 30.7 million) and seven in the South and West (total population 27.6 million)—shows a similar trend. Average densities per square mile outside central cities were 1,319 for the Northeast and Midwest and 498 for the South and West. Note, however, that counties in many western metropolitan areas include much larger portions of unsettled territory than do those in eastern areas.

The fastest-growing suburbs are almost always those at the edges of the built-up parts of metropolitan areas. These peripheral suburbs typically have densities much lower than suburbs closer in. Hence most new growth is occurring at low densities that generate more travel per resident than would higher-density settlements.

TABLE 1-4. *Densities of Large U.S. Cities, by Region, 1986*[a]

Region	Number of cities[a]	Total population	Total cities area (square miles)	Average overall density	Average individual city density[b]	Average city population	Average city area (square miles)
Northeast	22	12,846,880	960.8	13,371	9,147	583,949	43.7
Midwest	39	12,880,140	3,172.2	4,060	3,857	330,260	81.3
South	47	11,664,880	5,603.0	2,082	3,203	248,189	119.2
Southwest	27	9,794,860	4,497.4	2,178	2,390	362,773	166.6
West	47	14,079,490	8,116.2	1,735	4,585	299,564	172.7
United States	182	61,266,250	22,349.6	2,741	4,298	336,628	122.8

Source: Author's calculations based on data from Bureau of the Census, *Statistical Abstract of the United States: 1990* (1990).

a. Population of 100,000 or more.

b. Average population per square mile.

Preference for Low-Density Workplaces

Many suburbs—exercising their rights of local governance—require offices, retail facilities, and other workplaces to be housed in low-rise structures with low ratios of floor area to ground area. Such regulations cause jobs to become widely dispersed across a metropolitan area. This is what has happened in the greater Los Angeles area. By 1980 the nineteen largest clusters of jobs there—including downtown Los Angeles—accounted for only 17.5 percent of all jobs in the area's five counties.[15] In other words, 82.5 percent of all jobs were widely spread throughout the region.

Both local residents and building tenants like the adjacent free ground-level parking and attractive landscaping possible in such low-density work areas. Therefore, developers of suburban workplaces have typically found it easier to rent or sell space in these parklike settings. An exception is where workplaces are close to an airport, a regional shopping center, or similar amenities. Then more intensive use of the land with high-rise structures becomes a more important consideration than aesthetic effects.

Some jobs have shifted to low-density workplaces because computers, fax machines, and other telecommunications devices have made it possible to separate lower-level activities from executives without much loss of efficiency. Suburban office space generally costs less to rent than downtown space. So more firms have been moving operations to the suburbs, where lower land costs and aesthetic and zoning considerations encourage them to select low-density workplaces.

The density of suburban workplaces affects congestion because more new jobs are being created in suburbs than in central cities. In the fifty metropolitan areas where Coldwell Banker tracked office space in 1989, the suburbs attracted 72 percent of the new office space built and 74 percent of the office space actually absorbed.[16] Between 1970 and 1980 the suburban share of jobs rose from 46.9 to 52.5 percent in the twenty-five largest metropolitan areas and from 41.9 to 44.3 percent in all urban areas.

The combination of low-density settlements and low-density workplaces reduces the feasibility of commuting by mass transit. Such commuting is efficient mainly when many passengers' points of origin or destination are massed in a few large centers, so that routes and vehicles can converge at one end of the journey or the other. But when both ends of their trips are widely scattered, mass transit does not work efficiently. For the same reason, such dispersal also discourages use of car pooling, van pooling, and other ride sharing.

Some have suggested that dispersal of suburban workplaces decreases commuting times and distances by moving jobs closer to where workers live. In that case, low-density workplaces might have a beneficial effect on traffic congestion. Indeed, a 1980 study found that people who both lived and worked in the suburbs had the shortest average commuting time of all workers grouped by job and housing locations (table 1-5). But this does not necessarily mean that dispersed suburban jobs generate shorter average commuting distances. In fact, some suburban areas are so spread out, with structures separated by seas of parking spaces, that workers typically drive even when just moving from one building to another, thereby worsening congestion.

Desire to Travel in Private Vehicles

Most Americans prefer traveling in private vehicles, usually alone, because such travel provides convenience, comfort, privacy, and speed far superior to that of public transit.[17] This preference immensely increases the number of vehicles on the roads during peak hours, compared to more widespread use of public transit. It also

TABLE 1-5. *Average Minutes of One-Way Commuting,*
by Location of Residence and Workplace, 1980.

| | Workplace | | |
Residence	Central business district	Elsewhere in city	Suburb
City	24.9	20.0	26.4
Suburb	35.1	27.2	18.8

Source: William P. O'Hare and Milton Morris, *Demographic Change and Worktrip Travel Trends*, vol. 2: *Statistical Tables* (Washington: Joint Center for Political Studies, 1985), table I-80.

explains why public transit usage in peak periods declined between 1977 and 1983. By 1983 only 5.9 percent of all commuters were using public transit in the morning peak and 5.4 percent in the evening peak, whereas 88.5 percent were using private vehicles in the morning and 86.2 percent in the evening.[18] Any large increase in the fraction of commuters sharing rides could significantly reduce peak-hour congestion. Nonetheless, statistics show that close to 70 percent of all commuters drive cars alone. Clearly the benefits of doing so, net of costs, still exceed the net benefits of public transit and ride sharing. The commuter who drives alone enjoys not only greater privacy and comfort, but also shorter travel times, more convenient timing, and, if parking is free, lower day-to-day cash outlays.

To persuade more commuters to shift modes without changing the locations of their homes or jobs, it would be necessary to make net benefits of solo driving less than those of travel by other modes. That would require either increasing the net benefits of the other modes or decreasing those of driving alone. Unfortunately, it is extremely difficult to increase the benefits of alternative modes. So the most effective course of action is likely to be decreasing the net benefits of driving alone, mainly by raising the costs. A great many of the tactics analyzed later in this book are designed to do just that.

Future Trends

A recent analysis by Charles Lave suggests that traffic congestion in the 1990s will not continue to increase as it did in the 1970s and 1980s because its primary causes will have abated.[19] There will not soon be another baby-boom generation coming of driving age. The number of women obtaining driver's licenses will have leveled off in comparison with when they were first seeking independence and the percentage working outside the home began rising sharply. Also, household incomes will no longer be rising rapidly and allowing more people to own vehicles. In his view traffic congestion will not grow any faster than the population of driving-age persons.

Some of the data to support this view come from California. The ratio of vehicles in California "usable for commuting" (autos plus vans plus 57 percent of light trucks) to the total population of driving age (fifteen to sixty-four years) rose from 0.523 in 1940 to 0.76 in 1960 and 1.0 in 1986. But this rate of increase appears to be slowing as the ratio approaches or surpasses one vehicle for each potential driver. That seems to indicate true saturation of the population with vehicles. After all, every potential driver cannot drive more than one vehicle at a time. Lave also says that because the average number of miles each vehicle travels a year is relatively constant, congestion will stop intensifying.

But these statistics do not necessarily mean that congestion will stop getting worse. Even if vehicle use rises no faster than population, the latter can still soar in fast-growing areas. For example, the Southern California Association of Governments has forecast just such an increase in its six-county area. That region is already plagued by heavy traffic congestion, but its population is expected to rise by 5.8 million persons between 1985 and 2010.[20]

The suggestion that more intensive use of automotive vehicles will be less of a problem in the future is also questionable. According to the Department of Transportation, average miles driven per vehicle increased 22 percent from 1983 to 1990. If this trend continues, it will offset any stabilization in the number of vehicles per person of driving age. Moreover, although women now drive less than men, they might indeed catch up in the future. Since 1983, average annual miles per driver has risen 50 percent among women, compared with 28 percent among all drivers.[21] Further catching up by women would continue to intensify vehicle use. And because household vehicle ownership rises with income, if real incomes of low-income households rise in the 1990s, vehicle ownership will also increase.[22] Finally, since many households with multiple workers now have fewer vehicles than workers, more may buy vehicles to equal their number of workers.

This analysis implies that traffic congestion is almost certain to continue worsening in fast-growing metropolitan areas unless effective remedies can be found and implemented. Congestion may get worse in other areas too in the absence of such remedies. Moreover, the evidence suggests that many key causes of traffic congestion are rooted in long-established beliefs and behavior patterns. Any notable relief will therefore depend on whether these patterns can be changed through deliberate policies. That question is the subject of the remainder of this book.

Two

Strategies for Reducing Congestion and Four Traffic Principles

PROPOSED REMEDIES for reducing traffic congestion cannot be properly evaluated without some understanding of possible strategies useful for that purpose and of some basic principles of vehicle traffic that are all too often overlooked.

Two Fundamental Strategies

Congestion can be tackled by either supply-side or demand-side strategies. The supply-side strategy encompasses tactics such as building more roads that increase the carrying capacity of the transportation system. The demand-side strategy involves tactics such as encouraging more ride sharing among commuters that reduce the number or duration of the vehicle movements the system must handle during peak hours. Each strategy can be carried out through many different specific tactics. Subsequent chapters analyze separately the tactics associated with each of these strategies.

Two Basic Approaches

Another way to look at anticongestion tactics is to consider whether they rely primarily on voluntary market forces or on compulsory administrative regulations to achieve their purposes. Tactics associated with both supply-side and demand-side strategies can involve either market-based or regulatory-based approaches, or some combination of both.[1]

The Market-Based Approach

Market-based tactics assign monetary value to different types of travel behavior and then rely on travelers to choose among them.

Their goal is to achieve more efficient use of scarce resources, usually by making the prices of different travel options more nearly equal to their social costs so that marginal benefits will equal or exceed marginal costs. These tactics raise the price of the behaviors they seek to discourage in relation to the prices of those they seek to encourage.

Charging fees for using heavily congested roadways during peak hours is such a tactic. It leaves the choice of both routes and travel times to individual drivers. Another example would be to have employers pay each worker a travel allowance of $75 per month but also charge $75 per month for providing each parking space formerly furnished free. Employees who wished to share rides or use public transit could profit by spending less than their travel allowances on commuting. Those who still wanted to drive alone could do so by paying the parking charge.

The underlying principle of the market-based approach is that users of specific facilities should directly pay at least some of the costs they impose on others when using those facilities. Just one additional car entering a congested highway during a peak hour can add as much as one hour's delay to the total travel times of other commuters.[2] By compelling drivers who choose such behavior to pay for creating that cost, market strategies both discourage such behavior and collect money that can be used to compensate those on whom the cost is imposed. An example is by improving transportation facilities within the same corridor in which the money was collected. At the same time, the market-based approach permits travelers to continue socially costly behavior if they believe doing so is worth the price attached to it.

The Regulatory Approach

Regulation mandates certain behaviors or prohibits others. It does not attach varying prices to different behaviors, nor does it leave the choice up to individual travelers. Instead it prohibits or limits by government fiat the behaviors it wants to discourage and permits or requires those it wants to encourage. For example, prohibiting automobiles with license plates ending in the digit 5 from driving on Fridays, and those ending in other digits from driving on other specific days, is a regulatory tactic.

Advantages and Disadvantages of the Market-Based Approach

As an economist, I favor the market-based approach. Its advantages appear to far outweigh its disadvantages. Admittedly, nearly all its tactics contain some regulatory elements (for example, the choice of where and when to use road pricing is inherently a regulatory one that must by imposed by fiat). Therefore the most effective overall strategy for reducing traffic congestion should probably consist of both market-based and regulatory elements.

The principal advantage of this approach is that it leaves more choice to individual travelers. Therefore it is more flexible than regulations and requires far less enforcement effort. It is also economically more efficient because it seeks to equate the marginal prices of different behaviors with their marginal social costs. Although neither approach can achieve a perfectly efficient allocation of transportation resources, the results of the market-based approach are usually closer to that ideal.

Since the tactics in this category charge for the behavior they seek to discourage, peak-hour road pricing might raise huge amounts of money that could be used to improve regional transportation facilities Another advantage is that all drivers have the same set of choices, and groups are not treated differently, in contrast to regulation—such as the proposed California rule that firms with 100 or more employees allow no more than 55 percent of their workers to commute alone in their cars. The assumption here seems to be that large firms are better able to persuade their workers to act in this manner than small firms. Also, it is easier for regulators to administer a rule that applies only to large firms. Tactics that treat all drivers the same way apply not just to commuters but to all vehicles traveling during peak hours. In contrast, many regulations designed to reduce congestion apply only to persons making journeys to and from work and would not deter others from traveling during the most congested periods.

The market-based approach would also be easier to enforce, because it would require a smaller bureaucracy to administer, and its instruments would be more difficult to evade than most congestion-reducing regulations. It would be far easier to identify cars that fail to pay the peak-hour road price on a congested highway (as discussed in chapter 4) than to ensure that 45 percent of the workers in every large firm did not drive to work alone.

The principal complaint against market-based strategies is that they put undue stress on low-income households and hence are economically regressive and inequitable. Such households are less able to pay the prices imposed than are higher-income households. Some arguments have been put forth to counter this charge, but they have not been entirely convincing.

The Bay Area Economic Forum of San Francisco has stated that many low-income workers commute "against the tide" since they live near downtowns and work farther out. Thus they would not have to pay congestion fees traveling to work.[3] But this argument is not consistent with the commuting times of different income groups. In 1983 the average commuting time of households with incomes less than $10,000 was only 18.8 minutes—the shortest of any income group. Yet the average commuting time for workers living in central cities and working in the suburbs was 26.4 minutes. It appears that most low-income workers do not live in central cities and work in the suburbs.

Another point made is that the many low-income workers who already commute by bus would not have to pay congestion prices either but would benefit from the results. The question is, how many do use the bus? In 1983, 77.6 percent of all workers with household incomes below $10,000 commuted by private vehicle, whereas only 6.9 percent used public transportation. Even the suggestion that the money raised by road pricing could be used to improve transportation facilities used by low-income workers is questionable. A high percentage of adults commuting by public transit come from households with incomes of $20,000 or more—the figure in 1983 was 56.1 percent.[4] Unless the funds from peak-hour tolls can be used to compensate low-income drivers directly, road pricing may have regressive effects.[5]

Four Principles of Traffic Analysis

A vital point to recognize in evaluating remedies to congestion—whether they follow the market-based or regulatory approaches—is that traffic flows are influenced by four principles that are usually ignored. They are the principles of triple convergence, dual swamping by growth, the imperviousness of growth to local public policies, and one hundred small cuts. Many other principles of traffic movement are also important, but they are normally taken into account by persons weighing possible congestion remedies. These four principles are discussed in detail here because they have vital impacts on the potential effectiveness of specific tactics.

Triple Convergence

Nearly every vehicle driver normally searches for the quickest route, one that is shorter or less encumbered by obstacles (such as traffic signals or cross-streets) than most other routes. These direct routes are usually limited-access roads (freeways, expressways, or beltways) that are faster than local streets if they are not congested. Since most drivers know this, they converge on such "best" routes from many points of origin.[6]

The problem is that during the peak travel hours on weekdays, so many drivers converge on these "best" routes that they become overloaded, particularly in metropolitan areas. Traffic on them eventually slows to the point where they have no advantage over the alternative routes. That is, a rough equilibrium is reached, which means that many drivers can get to their destinations just as fast on other roads. At times, the direct road may become even slower than alternative streets, and some drivers eager to save time will switch to them. Soon rough equality of travel times on both types of route is restored at the margin. The opposite happens if travel becomes slower on alternative streets than on the expressway.

Several observations can be made about this equilibrium situation: (1) it tends to recur, because most drivers develop habitual travel patterns; (2) during equilibrium each limited-access road is carrying more vehicles per hour than each normal city street or arterial route because it has more lanes, more direct routing, and fewer obstacles; (3) many drivers time their journeys to miss these periods because they do not like to waste time in heavy traffic; and (4) at the peak of equilibrium, traffic on most expressways is crawling along at a pace far below the optimal speed for those roads, as explained below. Now suppose that the limited-access route undergoes a vast improvement—its four lanes are expanded to eight. Once its carrying capacity is increased, the drivers using it move much faster than those using alternative routes. But this disequilibrium does not last long because word soon gets around that conditions on the expressway are superior.

In response, three types of convergence occur on the improved expressway: (1) many drivers who formerly used alternative routes during peak hours switch to the improved expressway (spatial convergence); (2) many drivers who formerly traveled just before or after the peak hours start traveling during those hours (time convergence); and (3) some commuters who used to take public transportation during peak hours now switch to driving, since it has become faster (modal convergence).[7]

This triple convergence causes more and more drivers to use the improved expressway during peak hours. Therefore its traffic volumes keep rising until vehicles are once again moving at a crawl during the peak period. This outcome is almost inescapable if peak-hour traffic was already slow before the highway was improved. If traffic is going faster than a crawl on this direct route at the peak hour, its users will still get to their destinations faster than users of city streets, which are less direct and more encumbered by signals and cross-streets. Total travel times on these two types of paths will only become equalized if the limited-access roads are so overloaded that vehicles on them are moving at slower speeds than those on normal streets. Triple convergence creates just such an effect during peak hours.

Even so, highway improvements that expand hourly road capacity clearly produce social benefits. The total number of vehicles moving toward their destinations during each peak hour will be greater than before. If there has been no growth in the total number of persons traveling each day, periods of peak traffic congestion will become shorter because the system can carry more vehicles per hour. Traffic will now move faster just before and after the peak periods. As the proportion of all commuters traveling during peak periods increases, commuter welfare will improve, because more people will be traveling during the most convenient times. And peak-hour congestion on alternative routes and on public transit will decline because more commuters have shifted to the expressway. This might even cause the public transit system to reduce the frequency of its service if its total revenues fall. Except for this possible decline in public transit service, the region's traffic situation will be better.

Another possible effect of widening an expressway is that it will encourage more intensive development of the primary destination it serves—often an area's central business district. More commuters will arrive at that destination during each hour while encountering the

same degree of traffic congestion as before. Hence the road improvement may stimulate more real estate development instead of less
congestion, or some combination of reduced congestion and intensified development. However, this result does not occur in the short
run.[8]

In any event, expanding roadway capacity does not fully eliminate
peak-hour traffic congestion, or even reduce the intensity of traffic
jams during the most crowded periods—although those periods will
be shorter. In fact, it is almost impossible to eradicate peak-hour traffic
congestion on limited-access roads once it has appeared within a
nonshrinking community. In theory, such congestion could be eliminated only if the capacity of those roads were increased to the extent
that they could carry every single commuter simultaneously at the
peak minute at, say, 35 miles per hour or faster. In nearly all metropolitan areas, that is impossible. Therefore, expansions of road capacity—no matter how large, within the limits of feasibility—cannot fully
eliminate periods of crawling along on expressways at frustratingly
low speeds.

With one notable exception, any *initial* improvement in peak-hour
travel conditions on high-capacity roadways will immediately elicit a
triple convergence response, which will soon restore congestion during peak periods, although those periods may now be shorter. Such
improvements need not be made to the highway itself. For example,
if a new fixed-rail public transit system is opened, it will attract some
peak-hour commuters out of automobiles. That should initially reduce
peak-period traffic congestion on both expressways and normal
streets. But as soon as drivers realize that expressways now permit
faster travel, many will converge from normal streets and nonpeak
periods onto those expressways during peak periods. That, in turn,
will quickly overload those expressways during such periods, forcing
traffic back to a crawl. Peak periods will not even be much shorter
unless a new public transit system has drawn a great many commuters
out of automobiles.[9] There is no evidence that new fixed-rail public
transit systems in the Washington and San Francisco Bay areas have
diminished peak-period congestion on any expressways there. Other
factors were also at play there, however, as discussed later.

Similarly, if many people decide to work at home one or more
days a week, that would initially reduce peak-period traffic on major

roadways. But triple convergence would soon wipe out at least part of any resulting improvements in congestion on those roads during peak periods. All the same, many remedies to intensive traffic congestion are unquestionably worth pursuing. The point is that initial gains must not be considered permanent inroads on congestion—at least during peak periods. Furthermore, any realistic analysis of exactly what effects will emerge from proposed remedies must take the principle of triple convergence into account.

THE CONVERSE OF TRIPLE CONVERGENCE. The triple-convergence principle also operates in reverse. That means any factors that increase peak-hour congestion on limited-access roads tend to cause more auto-driving commuters to shift away from those roads in peak periods to (1) the same roads in nonpeak periods, (2) alternative routes during peak periods, and (3) public transit during peak periods. Such *triple divergence* has important policy implications.

Residents in fast-growing metropolitan areas are particularly eager to limit traffic congestion because they want to prevent further expressway traffic from spilling over onto adjacent local streets. To many residents, such spillover is just as great a concern as the time lost in commuting during peak hours.[10]

It is widely assumed that high levels of peak-hour highway congestion will stimulate public transit patronage. That is why many metropolitan areas have expanded, or are considering expanding, their public transit systems to relieve highway congestion. Yet those communities that have built new public transit systems have not experienced much—if any—reduction in peak-hour automotive congestion.

ONE REMEDY THAT AVOIDS TRIPLE CONVERGENCE. One proposed remedy apart from moving residences or jobs that does not suffer from the offsetting impacts of triple convergence is road pricing. If drivers had to pay relatively high tolls for using expressways during peak periods, congestion on those roads would initially fall. Moreover, the tolls would discourage commuters now using other routes, other time periods, and other modes from converging onto those expressways during peak periods. Hence peak-hour congestion on those toll roads would remain lower, although some drivers would be diverted to other routes. That is to say, triple convergence would be replaced by triple divergence: many commuters formerly driving to work during peak hours would be induced to shift to other times, to nontolled routes, and public transit, as explained further in chapter 4.

Dual Swamping by Growth

As already mentioned, traffic congestion is most severe in areas experiencing rapid growth in their total populations of people and vehicles in use. In fact, rapid population growth tends to offset the beneficial impacts of any particular remedies adopted to reduce traffic congestion. A remedy that successfully cuts peak-hour travel in year 1 by 5 percent will probably have no visible effects by year 3 if the number of vehicles in use is growing 2.5 percent per year. The added vehicles traveling each day will return traffic conditions to what they were before that remedy was adopted—even if the remedy is still in effect. Of course, conditions would have been worse in year 3 if the remedy had not been adopted and the growth nevertheless occurred. So that remedy would not be used entirely in vain.

Nevertheless, local residents will become increasingly frustrated if all the policies they support to reduce congestion—such as building costly new roads—fail to produce any perceptible improvements. Yet that is just what has happened in fast-growing areas such as Southern California because rapid growth swamps most such remedies. In many cases, it is part of a vicious circle: authorities improve highways to fight congestion but then those improvements create incentives to (1) increase automobile vehicle ownership and use and (2) change the location and form of both residential and nonresidential growth. Over the long run, these actions merely serve to intensify traffic congestion.

For example, construction of the interstate highway system and many other expressways in U.S. metropolitan areas was a prime factor causing more citizens to buy and use automotive vehicles instead of commuting by public transit.[11] Moreover, these roadway improvements motivated many businesses to choose highly dispersed locations along expressways. As a result, such workplaces were difficult to reach by public transit and railroads. So more shippers began to use trucks and more workers began to commute in private cars. As worker ownership of cars became more widespread, housing spread further into low-density suburbs, where public transit was even less feasible to use.

Road improvements were certainly not the only causes of increased vehicle ownership and use. Massive advertising by auto manufacturers, the federal provision of mortgage insurance for single-family homes, federal tax benefits for homeownership, and rising real incomes also played roles. Moreover, it would be inaccurate to attribute all the population and job growth along new highways to their construction. Growth within any metropolitan area is mainly the result of whatever forces are expanding employment there over the long run, not of specific new highways. The latter determine *where* growth will occur within the area, rather than *its total amount*. True, a metropolitan area well supplied with road capacity is a more attractive location for added jobs than one without such capacity. But that is only one factor governing the area's total growth. Nevertheless, past road expansions have surely contributed to the severe traffic congestion now plaguing many U.S. metropolitan areas.

Where growth is located also influences what mode of travel people use. If it is located along highways rather than in older, closer-in neighborhoods well served with public transit, it will generate more automotive traffic.

Traffic congestion resulting from rapid growth is extremely difficult to relieve if the growth has been caused by factors other than good transportation facilities themselves. The rapid recent growth of Southern California's population has resulted from such factors as good weather, proximity to Mexico and to Pacific Rim countries supplying immigrants, the presence of both a large low-wage labor pool and many highly educated workers, and the huge size of the local market. The attraction of these factors remains strong even though rising congestion has made local travel increasingly frustrating and inefficient. Hence these increases in congestion have not created any self-correcting processes. They are apparently not yet bad enough to discourage further growth by other factors.

Rapid growth can also aggravate spillover effects related to traffic congestion. Since 1970, public policies have tremendously reduced the amount of air pollutants discharged into the atmosphere in the greater Los Angeles area by each automotive vehicle, factory, and other stationary source. As a result the total air pollution there has fallen in the past two decades, despite a big increase in vehicle population. But these gains could be wiped out by the massive population and vehicle increases projected for 1990 to 2010. Authorities dealing with air pollution there already feel they are swimming against the tide of additional growth. Peak-period traffic congestion would also be affected.

The Imperviousness of Growth to Local Public Policies

The above analysis suggests that one way to prevent the quality of life from deteriorating in a fast-growing area would be to slow down its growth rate. That is the approach of "no-growth" advocates. Halting the area's growth altogether would indeed reduce some of the above problems, but such a policy would be highly impractical.

To begin with, no suburban community can hope to stop the growth of its metropolitan area as a whole if conditions favor the expansion of jobs there. A given community could ban all expansion of housing and workplaces within its boundaries, but that would not prevent nearby communities from accepting more jobs and residents. Every U.S. metropolitan area has at least some communities encouraging further growth. Even if none did, newcomers would continue to arrive anyway if they believed good economic opportunities were available there, as history has repeatedly proved. Such immigrants would either live on the outskirts of the metropolitan area in unincorporated places with no antigrowth policies, or they would illegally double and triple up in dwelling units within communities that had formally banned further growth.

These observations lead one to conclude that growth is impervious to *local* public policy. That is to say, no one suburb can substantially affect the future growth rate of its overall metropolitan area through its own policies.[12] Therefore, attempts by any one suburb to halt growth within its own boundaries simply divert potential growth, along with its problems, to nearby communities. Even then, the problems will not be confined to the places that generate them. They will inevitably spill over into surrounding communities, as is clear from the problems associated with air pollution and vehicle traffic.

Antigrowth tactics are especially difficult to sustain because growth generates economic benefits. As incomes rise, purchasing power increases and more money is spent in local stores and businesses. With more new commercial development, local tax revenues increase and reduce the property tax burdens on existing residents. Furthermore, added jobs provide income to many existing residents. Although growth also has its drawbacks—greater traffic congestion and air pollution are but two—completely banning further growth within a community imposes sizable penalties on many businesses therein.

Admittedly, individual communities can slow or even halt additional growth within their boundaries, and thereby reduce future increases in some negative aspects of growth. Hence local antigrowth policies do benefit local citizens. But, as already mentioned, such policies are essentially beggar-thy-neighbor tactics. They shift the negative impacts of growth to other people and communities nearby and certainly cannot prevent the problems that arise there from flowing back into the no-growth communities.

One Hundred Small Cuts

As many observers have pointed out, no one policy can fully remedy metropolitan traffic congestion. Indeed, most individual policies cannot even make a dent in such problems—especially in rapidly growing areas. That means various remedies must be combined to effect a cure. Those who are striving to do so are like the woodsman who must cut down a huge tree with only one small axe. He cannot fell the tree or even make much of a cut in it with one swing of the axe. But he can eventually cut it down, with one hundred or more small cuts. A multifaceted approach offers the only hope of reducing traffic congestion significantly.

However, even ten thousand small cuts will not completely eliminate peak-period congestion because of triple convergence. Hence congestion remedies should not be expected to eliminate the problem altogether. Rather, they should aim to (1) reduce the duration of maximum congestion appreciably, (2) reduce the average length of time required for commuting, (3) increase the average commuting speed, (4) increase the proportion of all commuters traveling during periods of maximum convenience, and (5) reduce the intensity of commuter frustration.[13] Rapidly growing areas may find it impossible to achieve any of these goals. Even so, they may be better off than they were before adopting their congestion remedies.

Part 2
Supply-Side Remedies

Three

Increasing Carrying Capacity

THE MOST intuitively obvious response to greater congestion is to expand the peak-hour carrying capacity of the area's transportation system. This supply-side strategy can be implemented through diverse tactics. However, their long-run effects are sometimes far different from what was intended; so they should be analyzed carefully before being adopted.

Building More Roads

Among the various supply-side tactics for reducing congestion, building more roads or widening existing ones seems particularly appropriate in areas that have experienced rapid growth. As their residents, workers, and vehicles increase in numbers, communities become more susceptible to traffic congestion. Between 1980 and 1989, for example, if a community's population rose 10 percent, the total vehicle miles driven there typically rose 43.2 percent; so congestion probably increased too.[1]

As mentioned earlier, rapid growth can greatly increase traffic loads on arteries throughout a metropolitan area, regardless of where it takes place. Consequently, remedial policies that reduce initial peak-hour traffic volumes by only a few percent—as do many demand-side tactics—can be swamped by further growth within the region. This is why many people think more transportation capacity is an essential response to the recent increases in traffic volumes.

Unfortunately, in the long run, building new roads or expanding existing ones does not reduce the intensity of peak-hour traffic congestion to any extent, particularly in rapidly growing areas, because commuters will quickly shift their routes, timing, and modes of travel.

37

As explained in chapter 2, the resulting triple convergence will bring congestion back to its maximum levels during the peak period, although that period may be shorter because of greater road capacity.[2] Moreover, if the metropolitan area as a whole is growing rapidly, the added traffic will soon overfill the newly built capacity, and the periods of maximum congestion will go back to their prior length. Also, the added travel capacity may help persuade more people and firms to move into the region, or it may cause more residents already living there to buy and use automotive vehicles.

When this tactic is used, however, considerable effort must go into the planning and administration of road building. Since the traffic in metropolitan areas flows over regional networks that go beyond the boundaries of any one community—except perhaps in the largest central cities—regional coordination of road-building plans and financing is particularly important. In fact, most state governments have regional road-building agencies within their own highway departments.

Making Transportation Systems More Efficient

Highway engineers have devised many ways of making traffic flow faster and more smoothly over existing roads. They are not designed to alter the total volume of traffic but to ameliorate certain problems that keep traffic from moving smoothly.

It is not within the scope of this book to analyze these devices in detail. Rather, they are merely listed to bring them to the reader's attention.[3]

—Programmed repairs and improvements aimed at properly maintaining existing expressways, highways, and streets.

—Coordinated timing of traffic signals along arterial streets. Traffic speed can also be improved 12 to 25 percent by replacing older traffic signals with modern computer-controlled signals.

—The use of multiple repair vehicles to rove major arteries during peak hours and clear accidents quickly. The nearest such vehicle can be rapidly radio-dispatched to any accident scene.

—Television monitoring systems along major roadways to spot accident tie-ups quickly and permit rapid dispatch of accident clearance teams to such sites.

—"Normal" city streets or major arterials upgraded to wider "superstreets" that also have partly limited access.

—Streets converted from two-way to one-way movement.

—Ramp signals to control the flow of vehicles entering expressways.

—Electronically controlled signs above expressways or regular radio announcements to provide "real-time" information on current traffic conditions for motorists.

—Street parking patterns changed to provide more room for traffic flows or shorter delays while drivers are entering or leaving parking spaces.

Combinations of these tactics can notably affect peak-hour times and speeds on congested expressways. For example, the Washington State Department of Transportation instituted a combination of ramp controls, television monitors, visual signals to motorists, park-and-ride lots, and added high-occupancy vehicle (HOV) lanes to improve traffic flows on interstate 5 in the Seattle area. After the ramp-metering program was started in 1981, but before the new HOV lanes were opened, peak-hour driving time on the main lanes of a 6.9 mile segment fell from 22 minutes to 12–13 minutes.[4] The average time motorists had to wait at signaled ramps before entering the expressway was less than 3 minutes. Over a six-year period, the entire project, including new HOV lanes, further reduced peak-hour driving time on that segment to 9.5 minutes and cut average ramp waiting time to less than 2 minutes. Yet total peak-hour traffic handled by all lanes in this part of interstate 5 increased by 86 percent northbound and 62 percent southbound.[5]

Using More High-Occupancy Vehicle Lanes

The greatest cause of peak-hour congestion is the desire of commuters to ride alone in their private vehicles. Peak-hour traffic volumes could be slashed if a large fraction of such "Lone Rangers" would carpool. One way to encourage doubling up is to set aside lanes for persons traveling in high-occupancy vehicles. "High occupancy" is defined as three or more persons in the Washington, D.C., area, but only two or more in Southern California. If HOV travelers can move faster than lone drivers, people will be encouraged to shift to HOV travel. Many areas have already established HOV lanes for cars and buses. But HOVs are still a small fraction of all vehicles moving during peak hours, with the result that these lanes are normally less congested than other lanes and HOV riders are able to move faster and spend less time commuting.

The basic purpose of exclusive HOV lanes is to reduce the time-saving advantage of driving alone, which occurs because picking up and discharging multiple passengers increases trip time. For example, people who value time highly are likely to drive alone, even though they might have to pay $1.80 a day in operating costs plus $5.00 parking, or $6.80.[6] This is much more than the $2.00 total for going by bus, which, however, would take twenty minutes longer each way. The commuter is paying a premium of $4.80 to save forty min-utes—which puts a value of $7.20 per hour on that individual's time (not taking into account the greater comfort and privacy of driving alone). Commuters who value their time at less than that rate would be economically better off taking the bus. If the time saved by solo driving was reduced to fifteen minutes, its implicit value would rise to $19.20 per hour. Undoubtedly, fewer people would value their time at more than that.[7] Thus the smaller the time advantage of driving alone, the more commuters are motivated to use ride sharing or buses.

HOV lanes reduce this time differential by removing HOVs from the congested "normal" lanes during peak hours so they can drive faster than lone drivers. Using HOVs also reduces the cash outlays of commuting, since basic operating and capital costs are shared. The resulting combination of a lower cash cost and a smaller time differen-tial may attract more people into ride sharing and using public transit.

The experience already gained with HOV lanes suggests, however, that congestion is not necessarily alleviated by shifting *existing* lanes from normal to exclusive HOV use. Instead, this reduces the overall peak-hour capacity of the road, because HOV lanes carry far fewer cars per hour—and sometimes even fewer persons per hour—than normal lanes.[8] Congestion on the normal lanes thus intensifies and encourages persons driving alone to cheat by driving in the HOV lanes. It also enrages thousands of lone drivers who find their commut-ing worse than before. When this tactic was first tried on the busy Santa Monica Freeway in the Los Angeles area, negative driver reac-tions were so intense that it was canceled within a month.

The best way to create HOV lanes is to add new lanes to existing roads, by pressing former shoulder space into use, or by adding more pavement. Instead of slowing down all other lanes, the new fast-moving HOV lanes will speed up traffic on normal lanes by drawing vehicles away from them.

Some crowded expressways have metered stoplights at entry ramps to slow down the entering traffic and thus keep vehicles flowing at, say, 35 miles per hour rather than crawling. The delay then takes place when gaining access to the road, rather than when driving on it. Where bypass entry ramps are provided into HOV lanes, such delays are not a problem, and the time advantage of driving alone can still be reduced without bringing expressway traffic to a crawl.[9]

Experience also indicates that HOV lanes need strict policing, at least when they are first created, to reduce cheating. If fines for invading HOV space are high enough and imposed often enough, solo motorists will be more likely to stay out of it. Another finding is that most people who use HOV lanes appear to do so because it saves them money rather than because HOV lanes speed their commuting.[10] This implies that HOV lanes will be used most intensively when many firms along the route are carrying out traffic management programs to persuade their employees to engage in ride sharing.

Since adding HOV lanes is a form of building new roads, it has the same limitations as any road-building tactic, except that HOV lanes can encourage people to ride more than one per car and thus have more potential for reducing traffic congestion than simply adding road capacity. But that potential is likely to be realized only if many people adopt HOV travel, which they are only likely to do if they are participating in ride-sharing programs sponsored by their employers. Otherwise, using additional lanes for exclusive HOV purposes may not expand total peak-hour capacity any more than permitting all drivers to use them. Hence the actual use of HOV lanes should be continually monitored and compared to normal use of the same lanes.

Building Additional Public Transit Capacity

Another supply-side tactic is to expand the capacity of public transit systems. Aside from a few large cities with extensive mass transit systems, public transit is not widely used for work trips. Among all work trips in U.S. metropolitan areas, public transit was used for only 7 percent in 1977 and 6.2 percent in 1983.[11] Public transit usage was even lower among workers living in suburbs: 4.6 percent in 1977 and 3.3 percent in 1983. Surveys have shown that less than 5 percent of the patrons and employees in the major suburban job and shopping centers at South Coast Plaza in Southern California and at the Denver Tech Center in Colorado use public transit, although bus systems serve both areas.[12] In Walnut Creek, California, less than 4 percent of the persons employed in office buildings *adjacent to its Bay Area Rapid Transit stations* commute on that system; the vast majority use cars.[13]

From census data, it appears that persons most likely to use public transit for work trips are those who (1) have no automotive vehicle available to their household, (2) live in a central city and work in its central business district, and (3) live in a densely settled community. Persons who fit into both of the first two categories had the highest public transit commuting usage of any groups, 71.6 percent in 1980. But all workers in the largest twenty-five urbanized areas who both lived in central cities and worked downtown—including those with access to automobiles—made up only 4.7 percent of all commuters in those areas in 1980.[14] All three of these factors are becoming less significant, however, because of recent trends in demography and settlement patterns. Those trends are highly likely to continue.

When even one car was available to a household, the fraction of its members living in the central city, working in the central business district, and using public transit dropped by half, from 71.6 to 35.1 percent. In contrast, only 12.1 percent of the one-car group working in the central city outside the central business district used public transit in the same period. Thus working in the central business district was an extremely important factor influencing the use of public transit. The percentage of all jobs within all urbanized areas located in these districts remained constant at about 8.8 percent in both 1970 and 1980.[15] But since 1980, employment in the central business district as a share of all employment has been declining in most U.S. metropolitan areas, as indicated by the spatial distribution of added office space.[16] Transit work trips are therefore becoming relatively rare throughout the country.

This means that even huge increases in transit commuting would not greatly relieve suburban peak-hour traffic congestion. Note that in 1983 only 3 percent of all workers living in suburbs commuted by public transportation, as opposed to 89 percent by private vehicle (including both drivers and passengers)—or twenty-seven times as

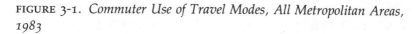

FIGURE 3-1. *Commuter Use of Travel Modes, All Metropolitan Areas, 1983*

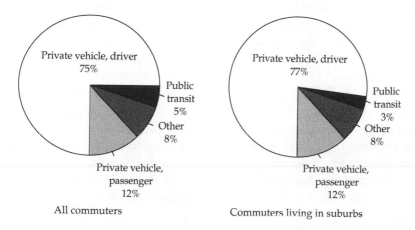

Source: Federal Highway Administration, *Personal Travel in the U.S.*, vol. 1: 1983–1984 *Nationwide Personal Transportation Study* (Department of Transportation, 1986), p. 7-11.

many (see figure 3-1). But suppose that public policy could *double* the number of suburban-resident commuters using public transit to 6.6 percent and that this entire increase came out of suburban automotive commuting. Such a drastic shift would reduce auto commuting by only 3.7 percent of its initial level. In fast-growing areas, this change would be fully offset by one to three years' growth in population.

Yet most policy changes alone cannot double the use of public transit. Some experts have estimated that (1) cutting transit or bus *fares* by 50 percent could raise ridership by 7–43 percent—with the biggest increases in nonwork trips; (2) cutting transit or bus *running time* by 50 percent could increase ridership by only 14–20 percent; (3) cutting transit or bus *waiting time* by 50 percent by doubling service frequency could increase ridership by 24–77 percent under various circumstances; and (4) all of these tactics would greatly increase transit or bus losses by either cutting revenues or raising operating costs substantially. None of these drastic and costly attempts to increase the attractiveness of public transit would come close to doubling its ridership—especially for work trips. Therefore, "from the transit viewpoint, it [would be] much more 'profitable' to gain riders either from restraints on automobile use or from increased density of urban development."[17]

These observations paint a discouraging picture for anyone seeking to reduce peak-hour traffic congestion in areas of high growth by increasing the capacity of transit systems. Even where large new systems have been introduced, peak-hour congestion remains a serious problem, as is the case in both the San Francisco Bay and Washington, D.C., areas. After only a few years, it has become difficult to detect any effect of these systems on peak-hour traffic congestion.

In the year ending June 1990, the Bay Area Rapid Transit system (BART) carried an average of 57,459 commuters moving each way daily. That was only 3.04 percent of all the persons employed in the San Francisco and Oakland metropolitan areas combined in 1990 (not counting the San Jose area). From 1985 to 1990, the absolute number of daily BART commuters increased by 4,738. But the absolute number of daily commuters not using BART rose by 209,260.[18]

In July 1990 about 9.54 percent of all workers employed in the Washington metropolitan area (including ten suburban counties) traveled to work on the Metro rail system, and another 8.5 percent used Metro buses.[19] Nevertheless, traffic congestion continued to grow in the Washington area, as demonstrated by the experience of Montgomery County, Maryland, mentioned earlier. True, many more vehicles would probably be clogging Washington area roadways if Metro rail had not been built.[20] Perhaps 10 percent of the Washington area workers added from 1985 to 1990 now commute by off-road public transportation, 10 percent by bus, and 10 percent by other nonautomotive means. That leaves 70 percent of these additional workers commuting by automotive vehicles. In 1990 these workers drove about 197,000 additional commuter vehicles each day that were not on the roads in 1985.[21]

Interestingly, the Metro rail system may have encouraged more downtown development than would otherwise have occurred. Metro rail converges on downtown from all directions, making it easier for workers to get there, with the result that the city center has become a better labor market for employers. But more downtown employment also means more peak-hour auto traffic on the roads serving downtown.

Since building new fixed-rail public transit systems is extremely expensive, most metropolitan areas are unwilling to finance the construction and operation of such systems without substantial federal subsidies. In other words, their citizens do not believe such systems are really worth the high costs they would have to bear to build them. Needless to say, expanding existing public transit systems—especially bus systems—is much less costly than building new fixed-rail systems. But bus systems must use existing streets and roads, unless new lanes are built for and reserved for them (along with other high-occupancy vehicles).

Public transit can also be expanded through light rail lines or systems. These usually operate on preexisting railroad tracks, or on surface tracks run in the midst of, or alongside, existing streets. They cost less to build than full-scale fixed-rail systems with underground segments through downtown areas. Partial systems of this type are now in operation in Portland, Oregon, and San Diego, but they serve only small segments of their entire metropolitan areas. Other light rail projects have been proposed in Denver, Los Angeles, Honolulu, and Minneapolis. Experience with light rail transit is still too limited to provide much information about its effectiveness. Yet there is no reason to expect such systems to be any more successful at reducing traffic congestion than full-scale fixed-rail systems.

Administering Public Transportation Systems

Whether all public transit within a metropolitan area should be operated by a single regional agency is not clear. Many areas have consolidated several privately owned bus lines into one publicly owned one. Some areas have also combined management of that line with the management of fixed-rail mass transit systems and railroad commuter lines. However, most such agencies sustain large operating losses that must be financed by current appropriations from state or local governments. In fact, most public transit systems throughout the world—even the most successful ones—require large subsidies.

Some experts believe public transit efficiency could be increased by reintroducing small privately owned commuter facilities serving narrow segments of the market. Such facilities include privately owned express bus lines offering luxurious accommodations to long-distance suburban commuters and private jitneys serving low-income neighborhoods. However, it is doubtful that these approaches would reduce peak-hour congestion to any extent, especially since they would use the same roads as auto-driving commuters.

Part 3
Demand-Side Remedies
That Do Not Change Housing
or Job Locations

Four

Peak-Hour Road Pricing

THE MOST controversial suggestion for attacking traffic congestion is that all drivers who use crowded highways during peak hours be charged a toll large enough to discourage many others from doing so. Some have complained that this would tax people for behavior they have never paid for explicitly in the past and would discriminate against lower-income drivers. So it has never been fully adopted anywhere. But now that congestion has become more bothersome and other approaches have proved ineffective, many areas are seriously considering this remedy as a last resort.[1]

The Economic Theory of Peak-Hour Road Pricing

Transportation economists argue that although persons driving onto congested roadways during peak hours are adding to collective costs by increasing delays for others, they are not required to pay the full costs generated by their own behavior.[2] They have to endure their own loss of time from congestion, but they are not charged for the time delays their entry imposes on others. So individual drivers continue to enter a roadway, even when the average total cost of their arrival exceeds the average benefit of using it. The Bay Area Economic Forum has estimated that a single driver entering the San Francisco area's congested roads during peak hours can generate one hour of additional delay for all other drivers there combined.[3]

As a result, peak-hour traffic on expressways typically rises above the economically optimal level—that is, the level at which the average total cost per driver (including operating costs, time, and any tolls) equals the average benefit to drivers of using the roadway. When traffic surpasses that level, it slows down even more; so the average benefit falls further while the average total cost rises above it. That misallocates scarce resources—both motorists' time and capital invested in road capacity.

The general welfare of all drivers would be greater if traffic could be limited to the lower level at which average total costs equaled average total benefits (see appendix A). This can be achieved by charging each driver a toll for using that road during peak hours. This *monetary price* should be set to bring the total cost experienced by each person entering a congested roadway up to the average total costs that person is imposing on both himself and others. That would be more efficient than the present use of a time price—delay—to ration scarce highway space. If every motorist who now uses those highways during peak hours had to pay a charge for doing so, many would be deterred from driving them. The higher the charge, the more people would be deterred. In theory, any desired level of peak-hour congestion could be arrived at by setting appropriately high tolls.

The reason most transportation economists advocate peak-hour pricing is not to reduce traffic congestion to the lowest possible levels, but to maximize the efficient use of society's economic resources, including both the capital invested in roads and the time motorists spend commuting.[4] Economists contend that such resources would be used more efficiently if more motorists could be induced to shift commuting from peak to nonpeak hours. Less commuter time would be lost through traffic delays, and roads would be more efficiently used over more of each day.

But such changes in commuter behavior would not eliminate traffic congestion or even reduce it to very low levels. Under these economically optimal peak-hour tolls, traffic volumes would be greater than at times when no congestion existed. It would still be worthwhile for commuters to enter an expressway on which congestion had slowed traffic somewhat, because that route would still be superior to others in that it is more direct and has no traffic signals. Therefore, even the imposition of an optimal toll would not end traffic congestion. Nevertheless, transportation economists are almost unanimous in their belief that peak-hour road pricing would reduce congestion substantially below present levels.

Although traffic congestion has been intensifying throughout the world, no metropolitan area has ever adopted a comprehensive system of road pricing to reduce it. Hong Kong tested a partial system for eight months but then rejected it. A few cities (Singapore, Oslo, Trond-heim, and Bergen) have adopted zoned peak-hour access tolls aimed at reducing congestion within their downtown areas, but no areawide system yet exists, in part because few transportation officials have been exposed to this concept, and so using it simply never occurs to them.[5] In addition, road pricing has been criticized for its inequity, inefficiency, and invasion of privacy.

Equity Issues

One predominant objection to road pricing is that it permits people with high incomes to travel at the most convenient times, whereas poorer persons are compelled to travel at less convenient times be-cause they cannot afford peak-hour tolls. Another is that road pricing is merely a way for the government to tax the citizenry. By charging money for something that was formerly free—travel on highways during peak periods—the government is depriving citizens of income they could otherwise spend themselves. This antagonizes people who believe that the government in our society is already too big and intrusive. These two issues are discussed below.

In 1983 about 86.5 percent of all U.S. households owned automotive vehicles. That included 60 percent of the households with incomes below $10,000, 91 percent of those with incomes from $10,000 to $20,000, and 98 percent of those with higher incomes.[6] Therefore, the number of persons who believe they might be inconvenienced by road pricing is vastly greater than the number who are sure they could afford the price of driving during the most convenient periods—which would presumably have the highest road-usage fees. In democracies, elected politicians are sensitive to the opinions of such a large majority. Most politicians are not familiar with peak-hour road pricing at all, but those who are have rejected all attempts to use it.

In practice, the strength of this objection will depend in part on how high the peak-hour tolls must be to reduce congestion signifi-cantly. But tolls might have to be made very large indeed to cut down on peak-hour usage of vital routes. New York City doubled its bridge and tunnel tolls a few years ago without any noticeable drop in cross-river traffic. It has been estimated that effective road pricing in South-ern California would require peak-period charges of 65 cents per mile in urban areas and 21 cents per mile in suburban areas. Those charges are vastly greater than the 2–4 cents per mile average charged on most existing toll roads.[7] If so, the typical nine-mile auto commuting journey would cost $2.92 in tolls each way—or $1,404 per year—even if half the travel was on roads without tolls. Few politicians will be willing to impose such costs on voters.

Some, like the Bay Area Economic Forum, have countered, however, that low-income drivers would not be harmed more than other drivers. These arguments are not convincing, for reasons presented in chapter 3. It has also been pointed out that money collected from road pricing could be redistributed to low-income households or drivers.

The effectiveness of these remedies would depend in part on how extensive a system of road pricing was adopted. The potential revenues from widespread use of peak-hour congestion pricing are huge:

> It is impossible to provide good quantitative forecasts of the effects of congestion pricing if adopted nationwide, but studies to date suggest that tolls on the order of $1.00 to $2.00 per round trip for typical congested commutes might reduce round-trip travel time by ten to fifteen minutes per commuter, raise revenue of tens of billions of dollars annually, and provide some $5 billion in net benefits a year to society.[8]

A third possible remedy is to spend the funds collected to improve roads or public transit systems. The latter could be substituted for peak-hour private vehicle travel by low-income commuters. However, many commuters cannot use public transit, since their trips do not start or end near public transit routes. Even so, it is argued that quite plausible uses of funds collected from road pricing, plus time savings from faster movements, could make all income classes of drivers better off, even after taking payment of the road prices into account.[9] The monetary value of the commuting time saved—especially after improving existing transportation systems—would more than outweigh the costs of the peak-hour charges.

Some economists contend it would be more economically efficient to channel the revenues from peak-hour tolls into general government expenditures than to spend the money mainly on improving transportation.[10] But many citizens see these tolls as "just another tax," and their hostility to them would merely be reinforced if most of the funds thus raised were added to general revenues. That hostility might be greatly assuaged if the revenues were directly linked to transportation improvements. When the money from new taxes is spent on the activity from which they are collected, the citizenry usually feels better about paying those taxes. Also, peak-hour highway tolls might have a better reception if they are seen as a form of user fee. Moreover, if some of the funds are used to improve public transit, that would provide more travel options for drivers forced off highways by the peak-hour tolls. Unless such links are established, it will be difficult to get political approval for any use of peak-hour road pricing in our democracy. Indeed, elected officials have remained reluctant to experiment with large-scale road pricing anywhere in the country.

Still another answer to the equity objection is that peak-hour traffic is becoming so congested that most people, even poor ones, would be willing to pay some price—including greater inconvenience—to improve it.

Efficiency Issues

It is also said that efficiency would suffer if drivers were charged time-based fees, which would either slow traffic to an intolerable level or would have to rely on unenforceable collection methods. The actual outcome would depend in part on whether vehicles could be charged peak-hour road-usage fees without disrupting traffic flows.

The latest technique devised to deal with this issue is called automatic vehicle identification (AVI). Electronic transponders are placed in or on each vehicle and electronic sensors on which peak-hour prices are to be registered are buried in the roadways. Computers are used to track vehicle movements, calculate charges, and mail periodic bills to vehicle owners. One such system has been successfully demonstrated in Hong Kong.[11] A small electronic number plate (ENP) the size of an audio- or videotape cassette is easily fitted onto the underside of any motor vehicle. The ENP needs no power from within the vehicle and can easily be removed, so the system will work only if drivers willingly leave their ENPs in place. Wire loops buried in or under the pavement of the streets on which vehicles are to be charged are attached to a cabinet-sized roadside electronic device linked to a central computer. When a vehicle passes over a buried loop, power from the loop energizes the ENP and causes it to transmit an identity signal back to the loop. This signal is transmitted to the central computer, which then calculates the appropriate charges for each vehicle, prepares a monthly or weekly bill, and sends it to the owner.

Another device offered a means of identifying vehicles that crossed the loops but did not have ENPs. Doing so is vital to catching drivers trying to use priced streets during peak hours without paying. The demonstration used closed circuit television cameras to photograph the rear license plates of any such vehicles. Once taken, these photos were transmitted to the system's control center, along with data concerning where and when they were taken.

This demonstration system operated for eight months in downtown Hong Kong. Careful evaluation proved it works effectively. It correctly identified more than 99 percent of the vehicles fitted with ENPs that crossed loop sites. All its key parts functioned reliably with low failure rates. The closed circuit television pictures were legible enough to confirm that an effective enforcement system could be devised so that it would not be necessary to stop every vehicle to collect a toll.

Although the demonstration system appeared effective, the Hong Kong government rejected broader use of road pricing, in part because citizens regarded the tolls as "just another tax," despite the government's attempt to explain how the system increased economic efficiency.[12] People also thought that such a tax, once established, would never be abolished and might even be increased to support nontransportation activities. In addition, citizens believed that the television cameras used to monitor traffic violations could also be used to track individuals whom the government wanted to arrest. This thought fueled fears that the Chinese Communist government, which will take power in Hong Kong in 1997, would misuse these instruments. Hence these objections might not be as powerful in other communities.

Although few cost-benefit analyses have been performed for road pricing, the costs of installing a system could surely be repaid rapidly through peak-hour charges themselves.[13] However, some practical issues remain to be resolved, as discussed below.

Phasing in Peak-Hour Road Pricing

No system for peak-hour road pricing could be installed all at once in a large metropolitan area; it would have to be phased in gradually. The first locations chosen would be road or other sites (such as bridges) that are heavily congested in peak hours and have no easy substitute routes.

How could motorists be persuaded to buy and install the ENPs? Since ENPs are not expensive, almost all motorists would be able to afford them. Transportation authorities would conduct an intensive advance publicity campaign to persuade commuters who used toll routes to install ENPs in advance of "opening day." Initially, these key roads would be modified so that vehicles with ENPs could travel without disruption, but vehicles without ENPs would have to pay peak-hour tolls at collection booths. Extensive pile-ups at such toll booths would soon motivate more motorists to install ENPs. Assuming ENPs were both inexpensive and widely distributed, most motorists frequently using these key routes would soon obtain them. Then only a few remaining vehicles—including those passing through from other areas—would have to pay the peak-hour charges at toll booths. This strategy would also call for the rigorous enforcement of heavy fines on motorists who do not have ENPs on their cars but refuse to line up at toll booths.

Another possibility would be "zone pricing," like that in downtown Singapore. Special fees would have to paid for vehicle entry during key hours in one or a few heavily congested zones—such as central business districts. Vehicles entering these zones then would either pay monthly fees computed by an automatic vehicle identification system—as in the Hong Kong demonstration—or buy stickers that exempted them from arrest and fines—as in the Singapore system (monitored by human spotters). Zone pricing would work best where congestion is heavy in a relatively limited and compact area (such as Manhattan) rather than over a broad region (such as Southern California).[14]

Dealing with Peak-Hour Traffic Diverted to Nonpriced Routes

There is considerable uncertainty about whether an electronic toll-charging system could cover all the roads and streets in a metropolitan area. If ENP detectors were placed above roadways instead of buried beneath them, it would be less expensive to install them on more streets.[15] The broader the initial coverage, the less traffic would be diverted to alternative routes not covered by the system. Where it proves difficult to cover all major routes initially, it would be wise to start with routes for which few viable alternatives exist, such as the Golden Gate and Bay bridges in the San Francisco area.

But many congested expressways are located near parallel streets on arterial routes. One expert firm has estimated that peak-hour pricing might reduce traffic on toll roads by 20 percent or more.[16] Since many drivers diverted from priced roads would switch to alternative routes without peak-hour pricing, traffic would rise sharply on those alternative routes.

This could offset much of the advantage of the reduced congestion on toll routes, if the system left many such alternatives untolled. Peak-hour pricing would probably never be installed on *all* alternative routes, even after an entire system had been phased in. Of course, modern technology changes so fast that some method of doing this might soon be found. Nevertheless, increases in traffic on alternative routes might become an almost permanent condition in the near future. Heavy traffic might therefore be diverted into residential neighborhoods or onto other socially undesirable routes.

An important question to ask is just how much peak-hour traffic needs to be diverted from toll roads to restore higher speeds there.[17] If reducing peak-hour loads by only a few percent would free up movement, then the volume shifting to alternative routes might not create intolerable congestion there. But if many thousands of vehicles per day must be diverted from expressways to restore satisfactory peak-hour speeds, surrounding routes might become seriously overloaded. A related question is how high to set the new road charges. They should be just high enough to divert the minimum number of vehicles needed to achieve desired average speeds, but they should not be so high that surrounding roadways become clogged because so many vehicles have had to be diverted. Choosing the right tolls will therefore be a matter of trial-and-error experimenting on each road.

Some transportation economists argue that the best solution is to introduce road pricing on all major alternative routes too. But it is probably impossible to install either AVI or toll booths on every street in a metropolitan area. Such a saturation strategy is practical only for main arterials and expressways, although it might be possible to draw a line across a territory through which many commuters normally drive each day and install automatic vehicle identification equipment on the main arterials crossing that line. The biggest problems would then be (1) to catch cheaters through some type of closed-circuit television system on all major streets crossing the line and (2) to prevent commuters from jamming up small side streets.

Thus, the practicality of peak-hour road pricing will vary from one metropolitan area to another. It will depend on their physical shape, topography, road alignments, and the volumes and nature of traffic flow within them. But in all of them, coping with the traffic that shifts to alternative routes that do not charge tolls poses a challenge.

Transient Vehicles and Traffic Diverted to Nonpeak Hours

Transient vehicles passing through a metropolitan area would not have ENPs and would have to pay peak-hour tolls at toll booths. Otherwise, they would be caught by closed-circuit television cameras and arrested or fined. That would avoid any administrative difficulties in billing them later at distant addresses. The likely delays at toll booths would further discourage transient vehicles from using these roads during peak hours.

Peak-hour road pricing would presumably motivate thousands of commuters to use the same roads at nontoll times. In 1983, however, the percentage of all weekday trips *per hour* in the United States as a whole was actually greater from 9 a.m. to 4 p.m. than during the peak hours from 6 a.m. to 9 a.m. At first glance, shifting trips from the morning peak period to later in the day would sharply slow travel speeds in later periods.

Fortunately, that is unlikely because of the uneven distribution of work trips in time. More than twice as many total weekday work trips per hour take place during the morning and evening peak periods as during the interim period. Presumably, a much higher percentage of work trips than nonwork trips would be made over the major expressways and other routes where peak-hour tolls would be charged. Hence shifting work trips from peak hours to other times would cause a net rise in the average work-trip speeds over each day as a whole.

How to Spend the Money Collected from Peak-Hour Charges

If peak-hour road pricing was widely used, large sums might become available for improving U.S. transportation systems. Some reports estimate that adopting congestion prices throughout the United States might raise $54 billion per year (in 1981 dollars). In large cities, net benefits might amount to $20 to $60 million per year.[18] Even after allowing for the costs of running these systems, this would produce substantial amounts to pay for improvements in transportation systems or to reduce present tax burdens for supporting such systems.

The Privacy Issue

Some people believe computerized vehicle tracking and toll billing systems would constitute an invasion of privacy if such systems enabled governments to trace personal movements throughout a metropolitan area. This was one of the main reasons Hong Kong rejected a broad adoption of road pricing.

However, there are ways to collect tolls without recording exactly where individual drivers are at any given moment. For example, individual cars could carry electronically sensitive "smart cards" on which a certain amount of toll charges had been prepaid. Each time they passed over a toll-assessing detector, the appropriate amount would be electronically deducted from their credit cards. When a credit card was exhausted, it would no longer enable its owner to pass detection points without tripping a "violator" alarm or having the vehicle's license plates photographed as violators. It would not be necessary to record which specific vehicles were passing over which specific detectors until the credit cards were exhausted. Drivers could protect their privacy by always keeping a minimum balance on their cards. This system already exists in Texas, Louisiana, and Oklahoma. In 1991, it was adopted by New Jersey, Pennsylvania, and New York for joint use on their toll roads.[19]

Subscribers could also choose to receive a nonitemized total bill, with details expunged from the system's central computers. This option is now available for telephone subscribers. Thus, the privacy issue need not be an obstacle to adopting peak-hour road pricing systems.

Privately Owned Toll Roads

Privately owned toll roads are yet another possibility. Only a few have actually been built, but many are proposed. However, merely because a road charges tolls does not mean its managers will set those tolls to reduce peak-hour congestion. None of the dozens of publicly owned toll roads in the United States uses peak-hour congestion pricing. All charge flat, nonvarying rates calculated to achieve revenue goals.

There is no reason to suppose private owners of toll roads will behave differently from public owners. Both are motivated to set tolls to service their debts, rather than to reduce congestion. Hence private toll roads will not have much impact on congestion. Nevertheless, one proposed toll road in Orange County, California, does plan to use differential peak-hour tolls.[20]

Other Effects of Peak-Hour Road Pricing

Peak-hour road pricing would also increase the peak-hour use of public transit because some commuters would find driving more costly than using public transit after taking into account all time, toll, and operating expenses. Furthermore, more commuters who formerly drove alone would start ride sharing, for the same reason. Both these effects would reduce peak-hour congestion.

In addition, peak-hour congestion tolls would affect land values, especially along the roads where such tolls were adopted:

> The burdens of a new tax or user charge are shifted throughout the economy through price adjustments. If congestion pricing were adopted, land values and wages would change as various competitive forces worked themselves out. . . . Owners of urban land are particularly likely to be adversely affected, and this would shift at least part of the burden from road users to landowners, making it even more doubtful that low-income workers will be hurt.[21]

Many of these long-run adjustments are unpredictable, so it is not clear just which social groups would gain or lose. It is doubtful, however, that these impacts would be large enough or clear enough to affect the political acceptability of road pricing.

Metropolitan areas that adopt peak-hour road pricing might also see an improvement in their competitive position if rival areas do not do so.[22] Every U.S. metropolitan area competes with many others to retain and attract jobs and economic activity. Peak-hour road pricing would improve its attractiveness by lowering peak-hour congestion. In view of the higher monetary costs of auto commuting during peak hours, however, it is not clear just what the net outcome would be in each area.

Would a Regional Authority Be Necessary?

Since the road networks in every metropolitan area transcend the boundaries of any one community therein, it would be impossible to plan and implement an effective peak-hour congestion pricing system except at a regional level. Also, it is unlikely that a purely voluntary coalition of local governments could make the tough resource allocation and locational decisions necessary for creating such a regional system. However, a state agency could perform this function by forming a subgroup assigned to a specific region and working with local authorities there.

Of course, peak-hour congestion pricing could be used in a limited zone entirely within one big city's boundaries. That is already being done in a few downtowns around the world. But this would not reduce congestion throughout the metropolitan area.

Testing Road Pricing

The only way to discover whether the potential benefits of road pricing outweigh its drawbacks is to have some daring metropolitan area to try it. The federal government should encourage such an attempt by offering to fund much of the initial expense in the first metropolitan area willing to undertake such a venture. The Intermodal Surface Transportation Act of 1991 calls for up to five congestion-pricing pilot programs, including areawide pricing. Until that happens, this most promising tactic will remain what it has historically been: a theoretically interesting device invented by academics but implemented only in their imaginations.

Five

Demand-Side Remedies That Focus on Behavior

A NUMBER OF anticongestion tactics try to change the way people behave within existing transportation systems and settlement patterns.

Shifting Peak-Hour Trips to Other Times of the Day

Many peak-hour trips could be shifted to other times of the day by staggering work hours among different organizations, adopting flextime policies, or having some organizations adopt four-day weeks. On an average 1983 weekday, 50.3 percent of all trips made from 6 to 9 a.m. were for earning a living, but they constituted only 8.6 percent of all weekday vehicle trips. During the 4 to 7 p.m. peak period, 31.1 percent of all trips were for earning a living, and they constituted 7.1 percent of all weekday trips.[1] Hence changing work hours would be slightly more effective at reducing congestion in the morning.

Even if 10 percent of morning work trips were shifted outside the peak period, that would reduce total morning peak trips by only 5 percent. So the potential for reducing congestion by changing work hours is limited, although this tactic might be worth trying as part of a larger strategy that also encouraged car pools and instituted HOV lanes. Changing work hours would probably not require a single regional authority, because it would be unwise to make such a policy mandatory for all employers. A single private organization could be set up in each metropolitan area to encourage more organizations to adopt varying work hours, but it should operate on a voluntary basis.

Encouraging More People to Work at Home

Many employees who used to spend every weekday in the office are now working at home part of the time. This enables them to reduce the number of trips they make between home and the workplace each week. If this trend affected enough workers, it could reduce the total number of daily work trips appreciably and thereby help to relieve congestion.

Computers and electronic communications have made working at home more feasible than ever before. They allow employees to transmit work done at home to their offices instantly and receive messages through telephone lines, modems, and fax machines. This permits "telecommuting"—acting as though one were at the office when one is actually working at home.

Despite the advantages of working at home, few people will want to work there all the time. Most people enjoy socializing with their fellow workers and find face-to-face meetings vital to maintain close links with their organizations. Also, people who want to be promoted need to be readily available to their superiors. Hence widespread home employment is likely to remain a part-time arrangement, particularly in view of the fact that employers believe they cannot monitor or control people working at home as closely as those working in offices or factories.

There are no reliable estimates of how widespread telecommuting has become. In 1983, 3.5 percent of all persons with paying jobs worked at home.[2] Suppose however, that T percent of all workers may eventually be able to spend either one day a week or half time working at home. The percentages of all morning peak-hour trips eliminated by various percentages of all workers telecommuting either one day a week or half time are estimated in the table on p. 63 (based on 1983 data).

Thus, telecommuting has to be common to make any significant impact on *initial* morning peak-hour traffic. Moreover, if telecommuting did at first cut peak-hour trips, some travelers now avoiding those hours because of congestion would start driving then. That would prevent the full initial reduction in peak-hour trips from becoming permanent.

Since telecommuting could reduce the total number of work trips

Percent of all workers telecommuting	Percent reduction in number of morning peak-hour trips	
	One weekday	Half time
10	0.86	2.16
15	1.29	3.23
20	1.72	4.31
25	2.16	5.39
30	2.59	6.47
35	3.02	7.54
40	3.45	8.62
45	3.88	9.70
50	4.31	10.78

each day, public anticongestion policies should encourage more people to work at home at least some of the time. Such policies could include liberalized tax deductions for expenses incurred working at home, efforts to prevent telephone companies from charging higher-than-usual rates for modems and home data transmission, modified health and worker compensation insurance policies to cover periods of working at home, and an easing of federal regulations that discourage home work to avoid sweatshop conditions.

Any drastic telecommuting policies would have to be administered across all or large portions of a state or metropolitan area, rather than within just one community. Similarly, tax policies encouraging telecommuting could only be adopted by state or federal governments. Therefore, no one metropolitan agency would be needed to encourage effective telecommuting.

Restricting the Days on Which Owners Can Use Their Vehicles

Some communities have considered restricting the automobile travel of people on certain days (such as Tuesdays) by ordering those with auto license numbers ending in certain digits (such as 1 or 2) to stay off the streets on those days. Violators would be subject to heavy fines. In theory, by assigning two digits to each weekday, one-fifth of all cars could be kept idle each weekday. Owners of grounded license plates would have to ride-share, use public transit, or stay home. This arbitrary approach does not take into account commuters who cannot easily avoid driving all five days of the week.

Encouraging Ride Sharing

The most effective means of reducing peak-hour congestion would be to persuade solo drivers to share vehicles. In 1983, 86.3 percent of all morning peak-hour commuters were in private vehicles, and 68 percent were driving alone. These lone drivers accounted for 34 percent of all morning peak-hour trips. Convincing large fractions of them to commute in two-person vehicles could substantially reduce morning traffic, as follows:

Percent of lone drivers during morning peak hours shifting to two persons per car	Percent of morning peak-hour trips cut
10	3.4
15	5.1
20	6.8
25	8.5
30	10.2
35	11.9
40	13.6

The problem is how to persuade people to double up. The number of workers sharing rides can be greatly increased by putting strong pressure on developers of work centers and on the employers located there to persuade their workers to engage in ride sharing. Such pressure can best be created through local government policies. One is to award a building permit for each new commercial building only if its developer agrees to reduce the number of commuting trips generated by that structure to a level below the number of workers it will house. Authorities could also monitor performance and pressure both developers and their tenants to comply.

Another method of encouraging ride sharing is exemplified by Regulation 15, adopted by the Southern California Air Quality Management District in 1987. It will eventually require all employers of

100 or more persons to encourage their workers arriving between 6 and 10 a.m. to reduce their use of private vehicles. Such employers must submit trip reduction plans to the Air Quality Management District for approval. Regulation 15 seeks to create a regionwide average commuter vehicle ridership of 1.5, with a target of 1.75 for downtown Los Angeles workers. That means 60 percent ride sharing among the latter.[3] More recently, California adopted a statewide congestion management requirement applying to all jurisdictions that share in recently increased gas tax revenues.

Such policies pressure developers and employers to form transportation management associations (TMAs) aimed at encouraging ride sharing and public transit use among their workers. Such associations adopt trip-reducing policies, such as the following:[4]

—Prohibiting free parking for workers driving to work alone.

—Providing free parking for workers using car or van pools.

—Allocating the most conveniently located parking spaces to vans or cars used in van pools or car pools.

—Allowing workers to adopt flextime hours so they can more easily share rides with others in the same building. However, flextime makes ride sharing more difficult overall in that it increases the dispersion of worker hours.

—Providing data centers where prospective car poolers from different firms can locate others who might drive to work with them.

—Providing vans at company expense for employees who will use them to share rides with other employees.

—Assigning a full-time person to supervise all ride-sharing arrangements and incentives.

—Providing free shuttle buses linking buildings to nearby public transit lines during morning and evening peak hours.

—Subsidizing fares for workers who commute on public transit.

—Persuading public transit suppliers to route buses or other transit services directly to, or adjacent to, a firm's offices or job centers.

Ride sharing can also be encouraged through tangible rewards. For example, ride sharers can be given the best-located parking spaces or be permitted to park free while lone drivers pay high daily parking fees. Surveys indicate that reducing costs is a stronger motive for ride sharing than saving time by using HOV lanes.

Ride sharing has been found to cut daily work trips by as much as 17 to 40 percent.[5] However, these are the greatest decreases on record, and they occurred where public transit services were available nearby. Hence such large trip reductions are not likely to prevail in much of a locality's workforce. Gaining a 10 percent reduction in trips through-out an entire metropolitan area by encouraging ride sharing would be an almost heroic achievement.

As the preceding table shows, a 10 percent reduction in lone com-muters would cause an initial drop in morning peak-hour trips of about 3 percent. But this small reduction is likely to be heavily offset by the subsequent convergence of nonpeak-hour travelers into that hour. So ride sharing programs do not offer great potential for reducing congestion throughout a metropolitan area. However, they might cut peak-hour congestion near a specific employment center if the trans-portation management association there was particularly successful.

A serious drawback of transportation management associations is their bureaucratic intrusion into their member organizations. To be effective, a TMA must pressure those organizations to shift their em-ployees into ride sharing and must also monitor their performances. Up to now, TMAs have mainly been formed where new job centers were being developed. Developers have strong incentives to set up such TMAs if local governments require them before granting building permits.

But what about employers in buildings developed before local gov-ernments adopted such regulations? They make up well over 90 per-cent of all employers in most areas, but are under no legal pressure to encourage ride sharing, unless their state or area adopts something like Southern California's Regulation 15. Even if their state or local governments adopt strong measures to promote ride sharing, it is unclear who will enforce those measures. To do so would require much greater monitoring of private firms by governments. Just getting existing firms to promote ride sharing strongly—when most have done nothing up to now—would require extensive outreach efforts. Who would provide them? How would they influence millions of existing organizations without a huge promotional effort requiring an extensive bureaucracy?

These questions have not yet been answered by the promoters of TMAs. No single TMA could function effectively across an entire metropolitan area. To do so, it would have to interact directly with thousands of immensely diverse organizations. That would require a massive effort almost sure to become bogged down in bureaucratic red tape. Therefore, a regional TMA makes sense only as an umbrella agency, offering resources and encouragement to many smaller TMAs in specific employment centers.

Even then, most existing employers probably cannot be brought into local TMAs voluntarily, unless traffic congestion becomes far worse. So effective encouragement of ride sharing seems likely only under two conditions: (1) where new workplaces are being created by developers, local governments can make building permits contingent on the formation and operation of TMAs, and (2) where the firms clustered in a single major suburban employment node tend to generate heavy local congestion and so have a strong incentive to cooperate in reducing it. But these situations cover only a tiny fraction of all workers who now commute by driving alone. Therefore, the potential of TMAs to encourage ride sharing is relatively limited.

Raising the Cost of Using Private Automobiles

Another way to reduce peak-hour congestion is to discourage people from making all automotive trips by raising the cost of driving. This approach is among those with the greatest potential—but is also the least popular.

In a high proportion of all U.S. households, workers drive private vehicles and the share of income they spend on transportation rises as incomes decline.[6] Therefore, increases in driving costs would be harder for low-income households to bear, both absolutely and relatively, than for higher-income households. This regressivity could be offset by reducing the auto license fees for low-income households or offering special rebates. Funds for such compensation could be raised from tactics that charge drivers more money—in the form of higher gasoline taxes or peak-hour parking charges. But there is no intrinsic link between such tactics and the way the money is spent, so there is no assurance such compensation would actually be paid. In spite of these drawbacks, the potential effectiveness of this approach makes it worthwhile to consider.

In evaluating whether state or federal taxes on the sale of gasoline or petroleum products should be raised, remember that U.S. taxes on gasoline are low compared with those in other nations. In 1988 the excise taxes on gasoline in the United States averaged 14.5 cents per gallon, for an average tax rate of 22.6 percent.[7] Yet until the conflict

FIGURE 5-1. *Gasoline Prices, Selected Nations, January 1991*

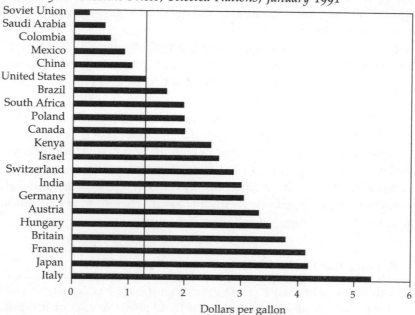

Source: Richard Homan, "Gas Peddled at Wide Range of Prices," *Washington Post*, January 12, 1991, p. A7.

with Iraq in mid-1990, the real price of gasoline—including taxes—had fallen in recent years. From 1975 to 1987, the price of one gallon of unleaded gas in 1987 dollars fell 27.4 percent, thereby encouraging more driving.

During discussions leading to the 1990 federal budget compromise, much attention was focused on increasing the federal gasoline tax, not to promote conservation, but to help offset the federal deficit. After heated debate, this tax was hiked 5.0 cents per gallon to 14.1 cents, but it is still puny compared with the gasoline taxes prevailing in most other industrial nations, whose gasoline prices are at least 50 percent higher than those in the United States—in some cases, even 300 percent higher (figure 5-1).[8]

What impact would a large increase in gasoline taxes have on commuter driving? The long-run price elasticity of gasoline used for work trips has been calculated as roughly −0.35.[9] If so, a 10 percent rise in the price of gasoline would cause a 3.5 percent drop in its consumption for work trips. In early 1991, unleaded regular gasoline was selling in the United States for about $1.30 per gallon, including taxes. To get a 10 percent drop in gasoline consumption for work trips, the government would have to raise the tax 37 cents per gallon. If the price of gasoline was doubled to $2.60 per gallon, its consumption would initially drop by about 35 percent.[10]

However, much higher gasoline prices would soon cause motorists to switch to cars getting better mileage. This would reduce the negative impact of higher gasoline prices on total driving. Even so, large increases in gasoline prices would probably be an effective method of reducing work trips, compared with many alternative policies. Although many commuters might have difficulty switching from cars to transit, because the routes they travel are not well served by transit, much higher gasoline costs might be still the most effective method of greatly increasing commuter ride sharing.

This tactic could not be implemented by either a regional or a local agency. Substantial increases in gasoline prices would have to be achieved through higher federal gasoline taxes or increases in world oil prices caused by external factors, such as the Iraq war in 1991. If individual states raised their gas taxes far above those of nearby states, they would encourage large-scale out-of-state buying. Only a uniform national gasoline tax increase could avoid subregional price and market distortions.

Political resistance to higher gasoline taxes would be lessened if citizens believed most of the money raised would be spent on improving transportation systems. That would be especially important if the tax increases were large enough to cause a notable reduction in work-trip driving.

A second tactic would be to increase the cost of owning a vehicle. In some nations, this is done through high sales or import taxes. In 1982, for example, Denmark charged a sales tax on a new mid-sized passenger car equal to 186 percent of the pretax price of the car![11] Or authorities could introduce high annual auto and light truck license fees, say, $500 to $1,000. This tactic would not focus on peak-hour driving alone; it would discourage all automotive vehicle travel. Such high ownership costs would therefore encourage ride sharing. But this tactic would be extremely unpopular in a nation where close to

90 percent of all households own at least one car or light truck, and more than 50 percent own two or more. These cost-raising tactics would also require action at least at the state level.

Raising the Costs of Parking

Many people drive to work alone because they are able to park free. The amount they save from free parking is often much greater than the gasoline costs of commuting. Moreover, free parking is an employer-provided tax-free benefit, whereas public transit travel allowances paid by employers are subject to income taxes. If free parking were prohibited, many workers would stop using cars for commuting alto-gether, and even more would stop driving alone. Five studies have shown that an average of 66 percent of workers drove to work alone when employers provided free parking, but only 39 percent did so after employers ended that benefit.[12] Shifts of solo drivers to ride sharing were much smaller when employers paid commuting allow-ances to all workers but still provided free parking.

Another way to raise parking costs would be to charge high fees on all vehicles entering parking facilities during morning peak hours, such as 6 to 10 a.m. Those fees would hit commuting workers but not most shoppers or persons running errands. To be effective, parking surcharges would have to be large. Otherwise they would not tip the balance of net commuting benefits away from driving alone to either ride sharing or using transit. This is clear from the fact that many workers now drive alone into congested downtowns in spite of high parking charges there.

Raising parking costs would be most effective in reducing peak-hour solo commuting where public transit services were readily avail-able. But even if no nearby public transit existed, higher parking costs would surely encourage more ride sharing. Such fees would motivate many solo drivers either to double up or to ride transit to reduce costs, or to travel at other times when parking fees were lower or nil. Hence such fees should reduce peak-hour work trips—but they have to be substantial enough and imposed on all worker parking spaces.

There are three significant differences between charging high peak-hour prices on roads and on parking. First, it would be easier to collect peak-hour parking fees. Parking lots are all in fixed locations readily inventoried and visited by tax collectors. Many commuters already pay parking fees, and those fees could simply be raised. Persons who now park in free spaces provided by employers could be charged through those employers. Moreover, high parking fees would not slow the movements of traffic. In contrast, charging peak-hour fees to cars moving on congested roads poses formidable technical problems. Collecting parking fees on the millions of parking spaces now provided free by employers would also create a sizable administrative task. This might generate a whole new bureaucracy that further interfered with the activities of many organizations, especially small firms.

Second, parking fees would be levied against only some of the vehicles using toll roads during peak hours, whereas road pricing would charge all such vehicles. Long-distance trucks or other vehicles making trips through a region during peak hours would not pay parking fees; so they would not be deterred from driving then. Nor would such fees hinder drivers running errands that did not require long parking. Also, if many commuters shifted to ride sharing or public transit to avoid high parking fees, then nonparking vehicle users who had been avoiding travel during peak hours might shift into these periods. That would offset some of the decline in congestion caused by high peak-hour parking fees.

Third, higher parking fees would penalize all peak-hour auto commuters, whereas road pricing would penalize only those who used those roads on which peak-hour tolls were charged. So parking charges would in theory be more effective at discouraging peak-hour commuting—especially if they were levied only against solo drivers.

The Bay Area Economic Forum has proposed linking the elimination of free employee parking to a travel allowance for all workers.[13] Workers could use it to pay for parking if they wished to continue driving alone, to pay some or all public transit fares, or to pay part and save part if they switched from driving alone to ride sharing. For example, if an employer paid each worker a travel allowance of $75 a month and charged $75 a month for formerly free parking, then workers who wanted to continue driving alone would be no worse off. But they could gain economically by using transit at a fare cost of less than $75 a month or by splitting the parking fee with others through ride sharing. Each employer would be no worse off if it continued to fill its formerly free parking spaces or rented them to nonemployees. However, employers would then be paying workers using the public transit system a travel allowance they do not pay now. So this scheme would be most attractive to employers whose workers now nearly all drive to work and enjoy free parking.

The impact of this policy on solo driving is accentuated by present income tax laws. They treat any employee travel allowance as taxable income, but do not allow travel costs—either parking fees or transit fares—to be deducted from personal income as business costs.

A milder form of reducing free parking for solo-driving commuters would be to end the income tax deductibility of all employer expenses connected with providing such parking. That would include capital and operating expenses for building and maintaining parking spaces used by solo commuters. Also, public transit subsidies for employees, or ride sharing and van pool expenses, could be made tax deductible. These changes would encourage business firms to reduce free parking for solo drivers and to increase their support of other means of employee commuting.

Another issue engendered by peak-hour parking fees is what should be done with the money raised? Those funds should probably be used to improve transportation systems in the areas where they are collected. High parking fees would be more politically acceptable if those paying them believed the money was going to be used in that way.

To affect commuting throughout a metropolitan area, such parking charges would have to be implemented everywhere therein. Although the specific surcharges used in different subregions need not be identical, they should bear some rational relationship to each other. Thus, parking charges in areas with the greatest congestion should be higher than those in areas with light congestion. But it may be difficult to achieve such coordination without instituting some complex administrative process for dealing with thousands of parking providers throughout the metropolitan area. If the rules, regulations, and general schedules of parking surcharges were uniform over the entire area, however, administration and enforcement could be delegated to local governments. Thus, only setting the rules, regulations, and general fee schedules, plus supervising their implementation, would require a regional authority.

All the tax changes considered above could be adopted only by federal and state governments, not by local or regional governments.

Encouraging Greater Use of Public Transit for Work Trips

Persuading more people to switch from driving to using transit could greatly reduce congestion, even if the transit consisted of buses using now-congested roadways. However, as discussed in chapter 3, convincing auto-driving commuters to use public transit is an extremely difficult task. Cars, light trucks, and vans are usually faster and more convenient than public transit, and always more comfortable, more secure, and more private. Moreover, the low-density settlements preferred by Americans are not suitable to public transit.

Investigating Intelligent Vehicle Highway Systems

Intelligent vehicle highway systems—so-called smart highways—have received significant attention recently. IVHS comprises several systems of electronic sensing, computing, and communications for managing traffic flows on major highways. In fiscal year 1992, under the terms of the Intermodal Surface Transportation Efficiency Act of 1991, the Federal Highway Administration planned to administer more than $230 million in federal research and development grants for these systems.[14]

IVHS encompasses three basic high-technology approaches to improving traffic flows. Advanced traffic management systems (ATMS) gather information electronically on congestion and flow conditions from many points of a highway network. They feed the information to a control center, which analyzes it and adjusts traffic signals, ramp entry controls, and lane direction controls throughout the system to reduce delays. Advanced traveler information systems (ATIS) also gather traffic data but feed the information to individual drivers before they leave home or as they commute so they can adjust routes and timing to prevailing conditions. Advanced vehicle control systems (AVCS) comprise devices on vehicles or in roadways or both that improve drivers' control of vehicles. Ultimately, automated control mechanisms could virtually displace drivers. Hybrid forms of these three ideas could be used to improve the operation of commercial vehicles and public transportation systems.[15]

The concept underlying both ATMS and ATIS is that better information about current traffic conditions during peak hours will enable traffic managers and individual travelers to make more efficient decisions that will in turn reduce congestion. This concept is probably valid in that quick responses could help avoid the traffic jams caused by the accidents and other unpredictable incidents that occur every day. But peak-hour traffic congestion is not caused by a lack of information. It is caused by too many people traveling at the same time on the same roads, mainly alone in private vehicles. Most are well aware that they will encounter congestion, but that does not stop them. Improving information about where congestion is worst will not reduce peak-hour overloading; drivers informed that route A is unusually crowded will shift to route B, overcrowding it too. All this means that heavy investment in improving drivers' and traffic managers' information is unlikely to reduce overall peak-hour congestion very much.[16]

AVCS might prove more useful in the very long run if the systems could enable vehicles moving at high speeds to travel closer together, thus increasing highway capacity. But advanced vehicle control systems are not likely to be practical on a large scale for several decades.

These conclusions do not mean that all smart highway systems are useless or not worth supporting. But they do imply that similar amounts of money, or perhaps even less, spent on implementing peak-hour road pricing or parking fees would have much more powerful—and immediate—effects in reducing peak-hour congestion. Because most IVHS concepts are still unproven in practice and may take years to establish, they will not be considered further in this book.

Conclusions

Seven demand-side tactics for reducing peak-hour traffic congestion have been analyzed in this chapter. Three are primarily regulatory, three primarily market based, and one informational. Each regulatory tactic—changing work hours, encouraging telecommuting, and encouraging ride sharing through transportation management associations—appears to have only limited potential for reducing peak-hour trips. None is likely to decrease such trips initially by more than 5–7 percent, although together they might cause a 10–15 percent initial decrease. But any *initial* reductions they caused would soon be partly offset by triple convergence. So their *net long-run* impacts on peak-hour congestion would be even smaller.

The three market-based tactics would raise the costs of driving during peak hours, either for all drivers—as with higher gasoline taxes or auto license fees—or for all commuting drivers—as with peak-hour parking fees—or for all drivers using toll roads—as with peak-hour road pricing. If these cost increases were big enough, they could make it too expensive for many commuters to continue driving alone during peak hours. That would divert more peak-hour trips to other times or eliminate more trips altogether than could the regulatory tactics. But that effectiveness would also hurt low-income commuters more than high-income ones, unless some compensation were paid to the former. Furthermore, only road pricing would avoid the possibility that some convergence would offset initial traffic-flow gains.

However, all three market-based tactics are politically unacceptable for most citizens and officials, mainly because they would impose large added direct monetary costs on peak-hour travel. The higher those costs, the more effective these tactics and the greater the political resistance to them. So advocates of these tactics face major marketing and persuasion tasks before they can get them adopted.

In addition, two of the market-based tactics would probably require regional legal and administrative authority. The other one, higher gasoline taxes or license fees, could only be achieved through state or federal government action. The regulatory tactics would also need regional authority if they were mandatory throughout a metropolitan area. However, they might be *administered* by local governments or private firms without becoming completely ineffective, something not true of the market-based tactics.

Part 4
Demand-Side Remedies That Change
Housing or Job Locations

Six

Remedies that Increase Residential Densities

A PRINCIPAL CAUSE of the massive amount of daily travel in nearly every U.S. metropolitan area is the low density of the residential settlements there. Because housing is spread over such a broad territory, people have to drive long distances to commute and perform other daily tasks. Therefore, many commentators have suggested combating congestion by increasing residential densities.

Social Benefits of Higher Density in Areas of New Growth

Settling areas of future growth at higher average densities than in the past could produce the following social benefits:

—*Reduce total movements required by the population*. This could have several ancillary benefits, such as reducing energy consumption, decreasing air pollution, and lowering traffic congestion. The last two would not necessarily follow from higher density, since they also depend on other conditions, as discussed later.

—*Reduce the costs of building infrastructure trunk lines*. Examples are major sewer, water, highway, and utility lines.

—*Increase the feasibility of using public transit for commuting*. Greater use of public transit would reduce total energy consumption and air pollution and could reduce traffic congestion under some conditions.

—*Make it more feasible to build relatively low-cost housing*. Medium-density housing units (low-rise apartments) are less expensive to develop than either high-rise or low-density single-family units.

Only the first three benefits are directly related to traffic congestion, so the fourth is not analyzed in this book.

These potential benefits can be assessed by comparing two ways of developing areas of new growth: first, at the average densities now prevailing in the metropolitan areas concerned, and second, at notably higher densities. The term *density* as used herein refers to *gross residential density*. It means the total number of residents per square mile, counting all the land used for any purposes in measuring each territory's area. This is different from *net residential density*. The latter is the number of dwelling units per acre of land actually used for residential purposes—excluding streets and all nonresidential land.[1]

The Marginality Problem

All strategies that raise residential densities suffer from one major drawback: they might influence additional future settlement patterns, but they would leave existing settlements largely unchanged. Because the latter are already in place, it would cost far too much to alter them extensively. Although some demolition of existing structures and subsequent redevelopment on their sites will occur in every metropolitan area, the vast majority of homes and workplaces that will exist ten years from today—perhaps even twenty years—are already there and will not be removed or drastically altered. Most additional housing units and workplaces will be built around the periphery of these existing settlements. It will be difficult for any locational tactics to have much effect on the movement patterns within such existing settlements.

It is especially difficult to change existing average residential densities. For example, if a metropolitan area containing 1 million persons has an average current density of 5,000 persons per square mile, it occupies 200 square miles. Of the 100 largest U.S. metropolitan areas in the period 1980–88, the 10 fastest-growing ones had an average annual population growth rate of 3.85 percent per year. At that rate, this hypothetical area would grow by 45.9 percent in ten years, or by 459,000 persons. Most would settle in newly built communities around the periphery of previously built-up settlements.

If the average density of these areas of new growth were *double* that of the initial sections, they would occupy 45.9 additional square miles. The entire area would then have an average density of 5,933 persons per square mile. That represents an increase of only 18.6 percent in a decade. To get a 50 percent increase in the overall average density within ten years with a 5 percent compound annual population growth rate, areas of new growth would have to be settled at a marginal density of 36,650 per square mile—which is 50 percent higher than the average density of New York City. That is extremely unlikely.

Why not raise residential densities in existing older areas too? As already mentioned, tearing down existing structures and building new, higher-density ones is very costly. Remodeling is less costly, but cannot increase densities as much. Also, residents of every neighborhood nearly always oppose major changes there, of whatever type. Hence they will strongly resist increasing densities in or near their neighborhoods, and they have the political power to do so. Consequently, local governments are not likely to permit substantial increases in density in existing neighborhoods, as proven by experience all across the nation. The only exception concerns up-zoning in neighborhoods near downtowns.

As for raising densities on vacant, in-fill sites in settled areas, most sites of this nature are too small to affect average densities significantly. Thus, it is extremely difficult to change average densities of an entire metropolitan area—including existing settlements—through either marginal growth or new in-fill development.

Reducing Required Movements through Higher Densities for Future Growth

Higher average densities help to reduce the need for movement generated by future population growth by accommodating that growth in a smaller added area than would be possible if development continued at the present average density. Consequently, the new residents would have to travel shorter distances to accomplish their normal tasks of living. That would reduce total energy consumed in traveling. Whether additional benefits from less travel would accrue depends on other factors. Less total travel would clearly reduce the total amount of air pollutants emitted. Whether this would in turn reduce effective air pollution would depend on locally prevailing ambient air conditions in the given area. Similarly, lower total miles driven might reduce traffic congestion under some circumstances, as discussed further below.

DIFFERENTIATING BETWEEN REGIONAL AND LOCAL CONGESTION. Both traffic congestion and air pollution in certain neighborhoods would be greater in areas newly settled at high densities than in those settled at lower densities because more vehicles would be owned and used per square mile. Moreover, under some climatic conditions, air pollutants generated in a small area remain there for considerable periods. It is easy for residents to conclude—erroneously—that regional congestion and air pollution would also be worse with higher average density. But both air pollution and traffic congestion often spread from their points of origin to other parts of a region. Therefore, the regional levels of these maladies are just as important to society as a whole, and perhaps more so, than their local levels.

REDUCING THE COSTS OF BUILDING INFRASTRUCTURE. Higher densities tend to shorten the trunklines required to supply areas of new growth with major urban infrastructure. Trunklines are the main channels through which utilities are delivered to each neighborhood from central stations, such as sewer treatment plants, water works, or electric generation plants. Trunklines also include expressways and other arteries joining the main subregions of the metropolitan area. Within each neighborhood, local feeder systems connect trunklines to individual housing units or commercial facilities. Changes in average population density do not greatly affect the costs per housing unit or commercial square foot of local feeder facilities. But they do reduce the total areas served by trunklines—and hence cut the costs of building them.[2]

This benefit arises from the geometry of circles, plus the fact that many metropolitan areas are roughly circular in shape. The formula relating a circle's area to its radius is: $Area = \pi r^2$. Population density is related to the area of a territory, whereas the length of trunklines is related to its radius. Therefore, increasing the radius of a circle by any given percentage increases its area by a much larger percentage.

The significance of this for trunkline costs can be seen from a hypothetical metropolitan area initially containing 1 million residents within a circular settlement at an average density of 5,000 persons a square mile. They occupy a circle containing 200 square miles; its radius is 7.98 miles. If the area's population expands 2.5 percent a year, in ten years it will have a total population of 1,280,085. Assuming the area retains a circular shape, how big it will become depends on the average density of added development. The greater that density,

TABLE 6-1. *Traits of New Additions to a Metropolitan Area under Three Population Density Assumptions*[a]

Traits of new area	Added population per square mile		
	2,500	5,000	10,000
Square miles added	112.0	56.0	28.0
Percentage added to original area	56.0	28.0	14.0
Total square miles in metropolitan area	312.0	256.0	228.0
New radius of metropolitan area	9.97	9.03	8.52
Percentage radius added	24.9	13.1	6.7
New average metropolitan density	4,102	5,000	5,614
Percentage change in average density	−18.0	0	12.3

Source: Author's calculations.

a. Assumes initial population of 1 million, average density of 5,000 persons per square mile, and area of 200 square miles. See text.

the smaller the added area. But the length of the radius will increase proportionately less than its total area (table 6-1).

The higher the density of this marginal growth, the shorter the radial trunklines would have to be. Thus, if the marginal density is established at a low 2,500 persons a square mile, existing trunklines would have to expand 24.9 percent to reach the outermost regions. But if the density were 10,000 persons a square mile, those lines would have to grow only 6.7 percent.

These hypothetical calculations are admittedly too precise. No metropolitan area is perfectly circular, nor does it expand outward in all directions at exactly the same rate. In fact, many are next to bodies of water or mountains that block all growth in certain directions. Nevertheless, the basic idea that high density permits lower-cost infrastructure trunklines is valid.

DENSITY OF NEW GROWTH AREAS AND AVERAGE COMMUTING DISTANCES. Appendix C presents a detailed spatial analysis of the relationships between settlement densities and average commuting distances. It leads to the following important conclusions.

1. Differing density levels in new growth areas have relatively limited impacts on overall commuting distances because most of every metropolitan area's future settlement has already been built. Unless a metropolitan area grows very rapidly, most of whatever development

will be there in twenty years is already there. So influencing the density of the areas added through growth will mainly affect traffic patterns in those new areas, rather than in the entire metropolitan area.

2. Average commuting distances will be much longer within new growth areas built at very low densities than in those built at medium or high densities. This is true even though low-density areas will contain more job sites than higher-density areas, because the former are spread out more. The model in appendix C shows that a large exurban area (defined as an outer suburban area, where new growth takes place) settled at 886 residents per square mile generates an average one-way commuting distance for exurban residents alone that is 21 percent longer than that generated by a similar settlement having 9,075 persons per square mile. Reducing the daily commuting of such residents by 21 percent over a long period would substantially cut the total miles traveled within a major U.S. metropolitan area. This is especially true in areas experiencing rapid population growth. Their new growth areas will contain a considerable fraction of their total populations by the end of the next two decades.

The exact percentage cited above is not important, for it is the result of a hypothetical model based on somewhat arbitrary assumptions. But this general conclusion has important implications for total national energy consumption.

3. The percentage reduction in average commuting distances achieved by raising residential densities is much smaller than the percentage increases in densities needed to achieve it. The 21 percent reduction in average exurban commuting distance mentioned above resulted from a 924 percent increase in exurban residential density. Another simulation showed that more than tripling exurban densities cut average exurban commuting distance less than 4 percent. One reason is that low-density settlement patterns also generate more widely dispersed job locations. Those scattered job sites reduce commuting distances for exurban residents, in spite of considerable cross-commuting.[3] This means that cutting average commuting distances significantly by changing densities in areas of new growth requires extremely large increases in density there. Small density changes will not have an appreciable effect on average commuting distance—even that of exurban workers alone.

4. The biggest impacts of changing densities on average commuting distances are caused by moving from very low to medium densities, rather than from medium to very high densities. Thus, moving from 1,000 to 5,000 persons per square mile would cut average commuting distances much more than moving from 5,000 to 10,000, even though the absolute increase in density is much greater in the second case. The reason lies in the basic way circular metropolitan areas grow. If 1 million persons resided in a perfectly circular metropolitan area, its radius would be 17.84 miles at a density of 1,000 persons per square mile, 7.98 miles at a density of 5,000 persons, and 5.64 miles at a density of 10,000 persons. The overall radial difference between the lowest-density case the highest-density one is 12.20 miles. But 81 percent of that difference lies in going from a density of 1,000 to a density of 5,000; only 19 percent lies in going from 5,000 to 10,000. Thus, from the viewpoint of conserving energy and shortening total travel, it is more important to avoid having new growth occur at very low densities than to have such growth occur at very high densities.

5. Reducing average commuting distances does not necessarily translate into reducing traffic congestion, although it may. Relatively long average commuting distances will not generate intensive traffic congestion if they occur in very low-density areas well served with expressways and other roads, employment sites in those areas are dispersed enough so that many workers do not converge on either a few job centers or a few highway bottlenecks, and the absolute number of daily commuters does not greatly exceed the road system's capacity to handle them. Furthermore, since commuting trips comprise no more than half of all peak-hour trips in the morning and less than half in the evening, changes in them affect only part of the causes of congestion.

6. Holding residential densities in peripheral areas of new growth above very low levels can contribute significantly to reduced traffic congestion there, but only if certain other conditions are also present.

Increasing the Feasibility of Using Mass Transit for Commuting

Another potential benefit of higher density is that it makes greater use of public transit for commuting more feasible. If many work trips shifted from private vehicles to buses or rapid transit systems, peak-hour traffic congestion would decline. An important study, *Public Transportation and Land Use Policy*, has concluded that the amount of transit patronage generated by the population living in any urban area depends on two sets of factors.[4]

One set concerns the characteristics of the residential area itself. These include its population density; the incidence of automobile ownership among its residents; their income levels, age, and average household size; its proximity to the central business district and the nearest other major business district; and the absolute size of those districts. The greater all of these variables except automobile owner-ship and age, the greater the propensity of local residents to use public transit, other things equal.[5]

The second set of factors concerns the characteristics of the public transportation serving the area. These include the proximity of the nearest rapid transit station, the frequency of transit service, its per-trip price, its speed, the other amenities it offers, and whether there is commuter rail service to the area. The greater all of these variables except trip cost, the greater the propensity of residents to use public transit, other things equal.[6]

Specific quantitative relationships among these many variables are myriad, varied, and quite complex. Consequently, separate estimates of transit usage must be calculated for each specific area.

The study on public transportation and land use policy also arrived at several general conclusions that should be mentioned here.

1. Improving the quality or quantity of public transportation service has limited potential for reducing traffic congestion, compared with either restraining automobile usage or changing urban densities.

2. Residential densities do affect public transit usage. At net residen-tial densities below seven housing units per acre (or gross densities under 4,200 to 5,600 persons per square mile), public transit use is minimal. It increases sharply at densities above seven units per acre. Therefore, "moderate residential densities in the range of 7 to 15 dwellings per acre can support moderately convenient transit service" (by rapid transit, buses, and taxis).[7]

3. In generating transit usage, the residential density of an area is less significant than its location. Residential areas near large down-town areas generate much higher fractions of transit trips than those with the same densities but farther out. Moreover, areas within 2,000

feet of rapid transit stops exhibit much higher fractions of transit usage than those farther away. Therefore, clustering high-density housing near either downtowns or rapid transit stops is more effective at increasing public transportation usage than raising average residential densities over large areas.

4. The density of nonresidential clusters—such as large shopping centers or business districts—is much more important in generating public transportation usage than residential density, other things equal. Hence clustering many nonresidential land uses close together would be more effective at promoting public transportation usage than raising residential densities but keeping commercial space dispersed. However, commercial nodes need 10 million square feet of nonresidential space or more to generate much public transportation usage. Moreover, to make bus service effective there, that space must be concentrated within not much more than a single square mile.

5. Sizable outlying shopping centers can support intermediate-quality bus service if the surrounding residential areas have net densities of 7 housing units per acre or higher. "Intermediate service" means one-half mile route spacing and about 40 buses per day, or one at least every half-hour. If 50 percent of the land is used for housing (excluding streets) and the average household size is 2.5 persons, then 7 units per net acre is equivalent to 5,600 persons per square mile.[8]

6. "The most important policies necessary to control rapidly rising transit costs are not in the area of land use, but rather in the area of labor relations" by keeping labor costs down. This is true because 70–85 percent of the operating and maintenance costs of public transportation are labor costs.[9]

7. Rather general relationships between residential densities and the feasibility of specific types of public transportation can be identified, although they are subject to great individual variation. By and large, these relationships imply that local bus service is feasible in even relatively low density residential communities, at the "minimum" service level of twenty buses per day at one-half mile route spacing; express buses are feasible in many medium-sized cities if linked to park-and-ride facilities; and fixed-rail services of all types are feasible only if they converge on relatively large downtowns. Rapid transit and commuter rail require particularly large downtown business districts.

8. At least two major shifts in public policy could enhance the prospects for increasing use of public transportation for commuting.

One is to prohibit the spread of new office buildings and multifamily housing through low-density areas. The second is to put more emphasis on taxing land and less on taxing improvements so as to encourage higher-density development.

CLUSTERING HIGH-DENSITY HOUSING NEAR SUBURBAN TRANSIT STOPS. Clustering high-density housing near rapid transit stops could substantially increase public transportation usage. Many households living within 2,000 feet of a rapid transit stop would be quite willing to use the transportation provided there for daily trips, including commuting trips. Some have proposed small, high-density pedestrian-oriented settlements served by fixed-rail transit, called "pedestrian pockets."[10] How effective such clustering might be in reducing suburban automotive traffic congestion is discussed in appendix D. The calculations there show that even extremely extensive suburban rapid transit systems serving many high-density housing clusters near their stops would carry only relatively small fractions of all suburban commuters. Creating high-density housing clusters around suburban rapid transit stops would produce relatively small reductions in traffic congestion, compared with the economic and political efforts required to both build and maintain the transit systems and create high-density clusters around each suburban stop.

A REVERSED CAUSALITY RELATIONSHIP BETWEEN TRANSIT USE AND DENSITY. Most of the links discussed above involve the effects of varied residential densities on public transit usage. But causality sometimes flows in the opposite direction. When many commuters into a business district use public transit, developers may be motivated to increase the district's nonresidential density. For example, when a new public transit system is built serving a downtown, more people can commute there without causing any greater peak-hour roadway congestion—hence without raising average commuting times. Yet commuting times influence workers' choices of where to live and work. If more workers can reach downtown in the same commuting time as before, more will want to work there. The suggestion that this may justify developers' building more office space or other facilities there is borne out by the huge expansion of office space in the downtowns of both San Francisco and Washington after the construction of mass transit systems serving them.[11]

Consequently, one way to strengthen the market for office and other space within a business center is to build more off-road transit facilities to serve it. That is undoubtedly why downtown business interests so strongly support construction of new fixed-rail transit systems—especially if they can obtain federal subsidies to cover much of the costs.

This relationship also holds for residential densities, especially in outlying locations. Thus, the better the public transit service to a residential neighborhood, the higher the density of housing that can be supported there, other things being equal. That is why high-density housing clusters have appeared around mass transit stops in Toronto and Arlington County, Virginia. Persons living there can commute by transit during peak hours without encountering highway congestion, and more people are encouraged to live near such transit stops than would live in those areas if the stops did not exist. However, for this relationship to bear fruit, local residents must permit previously low-density development near transit stops to be converted to higher-density development.

Existing U.S. Residential Density Variations by Geographic Area

Residential densities within U.S. metropolitan areas vary enormously.[12] These variations are partly related to the periods in which various U.S. regions were first settled. Since this chapter focuses on areas of new growth, the data of most concern pertain to suburban areas. Percentage distributions of suburban populations by seven levels of densities are shown for ten U.S. suburban areas in table 6-2. Seven of these areas are counties; the other three contain suburbs in more than one county surrounding a central city.

Total average densities among these areas vary from a low of 1,422 persons per square mile in the suburbs of Orlando, Florida, to a high of 5,884 in the suburban communities within Los Angeles County. Suburbs within Los Angeles County have much higher densities than the suburbs of Chicago within Illinois or those of New York City within New York State. Almost one-third of the residents of these Los Angeles suburbs live in communities with densities of 10,000 persons

TABLE 6-2. *Distribution of Suburban Residents, by Population Density, Ten Suburban Areas*
Percent

Residents per square mile	Illinois suburbs of Chicago	California							Florida		New York suburbs of New York City
		Los Angeles County suburbs	Cities in Orange County	Cities in Riverside County	Cities in San Bernardino County	Alameda County suburbs	Cities in Contra Costa County		Dade County suburbs	Orlando area suburbs	
2,500 or fewer	13.6	4.9	9.2	60.0	28.7	22.0	29.1		7.4	36.9	24.6
2,500–3,999	37.7	6.6	10.8	37.9	47.5	35.8	49.7		19.1	48.4	15.3
4,000–4,999	17.7	4.4	8.6	2.1	18.3	7.4	4.9		10.2	12.5	12.3
5,000–5,999	13.9	16.0	20.3	0	5.6	9.9	9.5		12.6	2.1	8.2
6,000–7,499	6.7	13.8	30.2	0	0	0	3.6		20.4	0	12.3
7,500–9,999	3.9	22.4	19.7	0	0	25.0	3.3		19.9	0	16.7
10,000 or more	6.5	31.9	1.3	0	0	0	0		10.3	0	10.5
Average density	3,482.6	5,883.6	5,129.4	2,003.3	1,934.2	3,526.9	3,344.4		4,844.0	1,422.1	2,557.7

Source: Author's calculations based on data from Bureau of the Census, 1989.

per square mile or more, compared with only 6.5 percent in the Chicago suburbs and 10.5 percent in New York City's suburbs. More than half of Los Angeles suburbanites live in areas with densities of 7,500 persons per square mile or more, compared with 10.4 percent of Chicago suburbanites and 27.2 percent of New York City's suburbanites.[13] Since Los Angeles is the center of the fastest-growing part of the United States in absolute terms, these data appear to contradict the conclusion that new-growth suburbs will not adopt relatively high residential densities.

However, the newer and farther outlying suburbs in the greater Los Angeles area, where the fastest population growth is occurring, have much lower densities than suburbs within Los Angeles County. In Riverside County, the average urban density in 1990 was 2,003 persons per square mile. No Riverside County community had a density as high as 5,000 persons per square mile, and 60 percent of the population lived in areas with densities below 2,500. Similarly, in the San Francisco Bay area, Contra Costa County—one of the frontiers of current growth there—had an average 1990 density of 3,344 persons per square mile.

These data indicate that U.S. suburban densities have until now reached relatively high levels only in older, closer-in suburbs, not in the more peripheral areas of new growth. Yet it is in the latter that densities would have to be increased sharply in order to reduce burgeoning suburban traffic congestion. Hence the previous conclusion, that achieving high residential densities there would violate the preferences of the existing residents, appears to be correct.

Are Low-Density Settlements "Socially Suboptimal"?

Defendants of suburban sprawl argue that if people want to live in low-density settlements, they should be allowed to do so—as long as they pay the full costs involved. From a welfare theory viewpoint, there is no reason for society to favor any particular suburban residential densities, as long as two conditions hold. One is that citizens choosing to live at low densities actually pay the full costs of their choice. The second is that those citizens do not create barriers preventing other citizens from living at higher densities.

DO RESIDENTS OF LOW-DENSITY AREAS PAY THE FULL COSTS OF LIVING THERE? Low-density settlements over large areas cause longer average commuting distances than would higher-density settlements with the same population under conditions widely prevalent in U.S. metropolitan areas. Therefore, low-density settlement generates more total automotive vehicle trip miles per day, which consume more energy and cause greater emission of pollutants. The consumption of more energy does not involve any clear-cut social costs, since those who choose low-density living pay for it themselves by purchasing more fuel for their vehicles.

But the discharge of more air pollutants is ambivalent. Because of variations in ambient air conditions, the emission of more pollutants does not always cause greater effective air pollution. But it can, and often does. Insofar as it does, and insofar as such pollution generates more sickness and other negative effects, the persons choosing low-density settlements are imposing a higher cost on society than would arise from higher-density settlements, without paying that cost. Hence the prices of different settlement patterns confronting households in markets will make low-density living seem more favorable than it would if its users had to pay its full social costs. This bias will lead to settlement patterns of lower density than is socially optimal. However, the resulting welfare loss varies greatly from one community to another.

Similarly, low-density settlements can generate more intensive traffic congestion than higher-density settlements under certain conditions. However, the relationship between average settlement density and traffic congestion is even more tenuous than that between density and effective air pollution. Low-density settlement only causes more traffic congestion if (1) the areas concerned are not well served with expressways and other road systems, or (2) job sites where workers from those areas are employed are concentrated in such a way that many workers must converge on either a few job sites or a few highway bottlenecks, or (3) the absolute number of commuters moving in these areas each day greatly exceeds the capacity of the road system. Under any of those conditions, low density is likely to create more traffic congestion than higher density. Then the fact that commuters using the congested roads do not pay for doing so will generate welfare losses that would not arise if densities were higher, or if all drivers had to pay direct tolls for using congested roads during peak hours.

Low-density settlements covering large areas also generate greater infrastructure trunkline costs than would the same population living at much higher densities. Some of these greater costs can be charged directly to the residents concerned; so they enter into the cost of choosing low-density living. However, most local officials claim that governments cannot fully recover all the costs of the public infrastructures serving new growth areas through charges against the new residents. Some infrastructure improvements benefit both newcomers and existing community residents in ways that cannot be disentangled through user charges or impact fees.

DO RESIDENTS OF LOW-DENSITY AREAS BLOCK CHOICES OF HIGHER DENSITIES BY OTHERS? Nearly all suburban communities have zoning ordinances that control the densities at which new homes can be built or existing ones redeveloped. Typically, these ordinances severely restrict the amount of land on which relatively high-density housing can be developed. That includes both multifamily housing and single-family housing on small lots. Analysis of this practice by many urban economists and by the Advisory Commission on Regulatory Barriers to Affordable Housing has clearly shown that suburban zoning often prevents the creation of higher-density—and therefore relatively low-cost—housing.[14] Many suburban governments pass zoning ordinances deliberately designed to prevent lower-cost housing within their communities. Their residents fear lower-cost housing located nearby would reduce the market values of their own homes. Also, they do not want to live near households of lower socioeconomic status. So they adopt laws that raise the cost of building new units, for example, by requiring relatively low-density housing.

Many residents of such exclusionary communities benefit from restrictions preventing the construction of lower-cost housing and entry of lower-income households because such rulings drive up the market prices of their own homes. In this way, they also attain the kind of local socioeconomic mixtures they prefer. But these policies impose costs on the low- and moderate-income households excluded from such communities. Since the beneficiary households generally have much higher incomes than the penalized households, this amounts to a regressive redistribution of welfare. In my opinion, it is therefore socially undesirable.

Insofar as low-density settlement is accompanied by the widespread use of such restrictive zoning ordinances, it reduces society's efficiency and welfare by inhibiting the choices of households that would prefer higher-density housing units. Such units could often be relatively inexpensive because units of moderately high density are less costly to build than those of either very high density or very low density.

Moreover, many low-wage workers employed in communities where housing is too expensive for them must commute from other communities, often driving long distances. Thus, restrictive zoning contributes to longer average commuting journeys than would otherwise occur.

THE SOCIAL OPTIMALITY OF LOW-DENSITY SETTLE-MENTS. Low-density settlements are not socially suboptimal if their occupants pay the full social costs of living in them and do not prevent the creation of higher-density settlements there. But in most U.S. metropolitan areas, many big low-density settlements do not meet these conditions, for reasons set forth above. Society would be better off if residents of these areas (1) had to bear more fully the costs their low-density choices have created, and (2) greatly reduced their restrictions on the density choices of others. Under those conditions, average suburban densities would be somewhat higher than they are now. This change would probably involve more clusters of higher-density settlements within basically low-density regions, rather than higher average densities throughout each region. However, the degree to which actual densities would be higher if socially optimal conditions prevailed is extremely difficult to estimate. Moreover, it would vary immensely both among and within metropolitan areas.

IMPLICATIONS FOR REDUCING TRAFFIC CONGESTION. Even if existing U.S. settlements had socially suboptimal densities, raising their densities would not necessarily reduce existing traffic congestion. And the difficulties of raising densities are great. In fact, trying to decrease current traffic congestion by raising residential densities in existing suburbs is like trying to improve the position of a painting hung too high on the living room wall by jacking up the ceiling instead of moving the painting. The effort required by the remedy is wholly disproportionate to the severity of the problem, the pain it is causing, and the benefits of ending it.

However, trying to reduce *future* traffic congestion in potential new growth areas might justify adopting some minimum average density levels so as to reduce the average length of future commuting trips there.

How Higher Residential Densities Might Be Achieved

In theory, there are three ways to attain higher suburban densities: by demolishing existing structures and redeveloping the cleared land with more intensive uses, or modifying existing structures; by building new structures on vacant, in-fill sites at higher densities than in sur-rounding development; and by creating new peripheral developments on vacant land at higher densities than the average for regions that are already built up. But only the third method has shown much promise of greatly changing the future overall density of a metropoli-tan area.

Densities can be raised on vacant peripheral land by (1) using smaller lots for detached single-family homes, (2) allocating a higher percentage of all residentially zoned vacant land to multifamily or attached single-family housing, (3) raising the permissible densities for such housing, and (4) allocating a higher percentage of total land area to residential uses. All of these policies can be legally imposed by local zoning regulations.

However, the first three are normally opposed by existing residents, who tend to believe those tactics undesirably "change the established character" of their communities. They fear greater traffic congestion, shortages of on-street parking, greater noise and air pollution, lower property values of nearby single-family homes, overloading of public facilities such as parks and schools, and the introduction of "undesir-able people." Thus, higher-density housing is considered a LULU by existing residents, who therefore adopt a NIMBY attitude toward it.[15]

It is hard to overcome this parochial response by persuading local governments to permit higher-density development. Most local gov-ernments have strong incentives to support the land-use preferences of their own citizens, while ignoring the needs of the metropolitan area as a whole. Hence the best ways to encourage higher-density development in areas of new growth is through policies adopted by territorially broader levels of government—especially the state. State officials have constituencies that often encompass an entire metropoli-tan area, including many potential residents of areas of new growth. These persons would benefit from lower-cost housing and other fruits of higher-density development. Sensitive to this fact, officials at broader levels of government are more likely to adopt policies that take into account areawide or societywide interests than officials in fragmented local governments.[16]

One such policy would be to revise property taxes so they fell much more heavily on land than on improvements. This would encourage maximum-intensity development of each site. A second policy would be to greatly increase property taxes on vacant land near the edges of a metropolitan area. In many states, such vacant land is now taxed relatively lightly, especially if classified as agricultural. Higher land taxes would motivate owners of such land to develop it quickly as intensively as possible, rather than hold it vacant while speculating on future value increases.

However, the impacts of these policies would be limited because most suburbs already tightly ration high-intensity land uses through restrictive zoning. This creates a shortage of high-intensity uses and drives up the costs of building high-density developments. Thus, the major factor preventing more high-density development in most suburbs is not the lack of tax incentives but the inability to get local permission to build it. Consequently, the way to achieve higher average densities in areas of new growth is to change suburban zoning policies. The details of how that might be done are beyond the scope of this book.

Another way to raise peripheral densities would be to adopt an urban growth boundary. It would force most new development into zones contiguous to territory already built up. Oregon has followed this policy for more than a decade. It has raised average densities in areas of new growth within such boundaries.[17]

One of the biggest advantages of urban growth boundaries is that they reduce the "leap-frog" development that initially bypasses large vacant sites in mostly developed territory. Leap-frog development raises trunkline infrastructure costs, in comparison with solid, contiguous development. Moreover, when new development is confined to well-defined territories lying within urban growth boundaries, uncertainties about future growth patterns are reduced. This permits developers and local governments to shorten the time required for planning and gaining government permissions for new projects. The resulting decreases in development costs can offset the higher prices of land within urban growth boundaries.

But reducing leap-frog development also has negative effects. Such development creates pockets of undeveloped land that stand vacant after the frontier of development has passed beyond them. If initial development of those sites is deferred long enough, they will eventually be improved at higher densities than would have prevailed if they had been developed when at the frontier.[18]

Another tactic to help achieve higher densities in areas of new growth is to provide persuasive evidence that well-designed, moderate-density, new multifamily residential developments would not negatively affect the market value of nearby single-family homes. The Advisory Commission on Regulatory Barriers to Affordable Housing found fifteen relevant studies of this topic. Fourteen "reached the conclusion that there are no significant negative effects from locating subsidized, special-purpose, or manufactured housing near market-rate developments."[19]

Clearly, overcoming current suburban resistance to higher-density development will not be easy. It can probably be done only if officials at higher levels of government, especially at the state level, become convinced that the benefits of higher density are worth the political costs of achieving it.

Seven

Changing the Jobs-Housing Balance

O NE STRATEGY for reducing congestion focuses on changing the balance between jobs and housing within each subregion of a metropolitan area. The basic idea is to encourage people to live closer to where they work and thereby shorten average commuting journeys.

The Nature of Jobs-Housing Imbalances

Under quite common circumstances, long average commuting journeys generate more traffic congestion than shorter ones. Long journeys often result from imbalances between job sites and the places people reside. Many more jobs than housing units tend to be concentrated in areas with a job surplus or housing shortage. These areas include most downtown business districts, large retail and office clusters around big regional shopping centers, and office and industrial facilities surrounding regional airports. Many people who work there must commute from relatively distant residences.[1]

Areas with a job shortage or housing surplus tend to have many more housing units than jobs. They are mainly outlying suburbs at the frontier of new growth where land is relatively inexpensive and so housing costs less than in areas closer in. That attracts low- and moderate-income households or those who want large homes without paying immense prices. Many people living there must commute relatively long distances to reach their jobs.

Even if the number of housing units in an area is exactly the same as that required to house everyone who works there, the cost and styles of those housing units may not be appropriate for those workers. For example, low-wage workers employed in a regional shopping center may be unable to afford any nearby housing if exclusionary zoning keeps the prices high. Hence an effective jobs-housing balance can only be achieved by closely matching both the number of local housing units and the prices and styles of those units to the number and economic capabilities of locally employed workers.

There is little doubt that such jobs-housing imbalances are widespread within large U.S. metropolitan areas. When the ratio of workers employed to workers residing in twenty-two San Francisco Bay area cities was calculated, it was found that the average ratio was 1.05—nearly perfect balance (any ratio between 0.75 and 1.50 was assumed to indicate reasonable local balance). Seven of the twenty-two cities had ratios outside this range.[2] Both results partly reflect the fact that, the smaller the territory surveyed, the greater the probability its jobs and housing will not be balanced. Conversely, over any whole region, jobs and housing are always balanced by definition (except for the few workers who commute in from outside it or who live in it but work outside).

Such imbalances probably do contribute to traffic congestion. However, their mere existence does not prove they are socially undesirable, that they could be removed through public policies, or that altering them would greatly reduce traffic congestion. These issues are examined in the remainder of this chapter.

Some Undesirable Effects of Imbalances

In theory, if more housing units were located in areas with a job surplus and more jobs in areas with a housing surplus, workers would live closer to their jobs, and total commuting travel would decline. Therefore, one strategy for reducing traffic congestion is to adjust existing or proposed future settlement patterns to approach a jobs-housing balance.

The importance attributed to this strategy can be seen from calculations of future traffic congestion made by the Southern California Association of Governments (SCAG). Projections in 1986 indicated that the population of the six-county SCAG area was likely to increase by 5.9 million, or 47.5 percent, between 1984 and 2010. In that period, the region would add about 3 million jobs—but not where its new housing would be created. As a result, traffic congestion within SCAG's region was projected to increase drastically to near-paralysis levels.

One way to mitigate that adverse effect would be to build many miles of additional freeways. But SCAG concluded that such action would cost much more than could be financed. Another approach would be to change the projected locations of added jobs and housing units. If 12 percent of the new jobs were shifted from areas of job surplus to areas of housing surplus, and 6 percent of the new housing units from areas of housing surplus to those with a job surplus, the projected increase in traffic congestion would be cut 35 percent. Hence SCAG adopted an official policy of influencing the future location of jobs and housing.[3] The required direct government intervention in the locational choices of private firms and households would be a radical departure from past public policies.

The Causes of Imbalances

Jobs-housing imbalances are the result of both the inherent dynamics of metropolitan-area growth and specific public policies that could be changed.

THE DYNAMICS OF METROPOLITAN-AREA GROWTH. When a metropolitan area is first established, jobs cluster near its center. That location provides greater access to all points within the area than any other spot. Such accessibility enables many firms to tap both wider markets and bigger labor pools. Moreover, they cluster together to improve the efficiency of their interactions and thus can pay higher rents for high-access central land than homeowners. Consequently, residential uses move to the outer edges of the developed area, where land is less costly. This automatically creates regions with both a job surplus and a housing surplus. Hence significant jobs-housing imbalances are socially efficient results of the "normal" urban development process.

At first, commuting distances between these specialized regions are short. But as the entire area grows, they become longer. Also, many retail and other services closely tied to daily household living move to peripheral sites to get closer to their customers, often creating new decentralized job centers. In this way, more jobs gradually move out into areas with a housing surplus, reducing initial jobs-housing imbalances there. Some offices and industrial firms also move to where workers reside in order to more easily tap the labor pools there. This process has also been furthered by rapid expansion of automotive vehicle ownership and usage since 1970 and recent advances in tele-communications. This evolution can be observed in Orange County, California, from 1940 to 1988. In 1974, the county had 37 percent more resident workers than local jobs. But by 1988, it contained only 18 percent more resident workers than local jobs.[4] Thus, a "natural" process tends to reduce initial housing surpluses in once-outlying areas over time as new growth passes beyond them.

This gradual leveling off of initial jobs-housing imbalances is strengthened by individual adjustments to long commuting journeys. People dissatisfied with such journeys often change home locations or jobs. It has been said that is why average automotive commuting times actually fell from 1980 to 1985 in eighteen of the country's twenty largest metropolitan areas.[5]

TRAVEL COSTS LESS THAN LAND. One factor operating against this equilibrating process is that travel is less costly to the average household than land or housing. The average household spends 16.7 percent of its annual income for transportation, not count-ing the cost of time spent in traveling. But it spends 26 percent for housing.[6] Therefore it can benefit if it can greatly reduce its housing costs by increasing its transportation costs somewhat. Commuting farther out can sharply reduce costs because peripheral land is so much less expensive.[7] The main added transportation cost is the value of the additional time required. Traveling 10 miles farther—which would double the average commuting journey—would increase an-nual work-trip travel by 4,400 miles. At 10 cents per mile operating costs, that is only $440. If the trip took twenty minutes more each way, and time was valued at $10.00 per hour, that would add $1,468 more.[8] Capitalized at 10 percent, this total added annual cost would equal $19,080, or $954 per additional mile of commuting each way. If a household can save more than that on the price of a given quality house by accepting a longer commute, it gains economically.

This is why so many households are making very long commuting journeys in high-housing-cost metropolitan areas such as Los Angeles and San Francisco. These relationships tend to maintain housing sur-pluses in subregions on the edges of each metropolitan area. Only after such regions have been bypassed by further growth will they naturally begin to shift toward a more even jobs-housing balance.

LABOR MARKET FACTORS. Because of the long-run increase in the number of women working outside the home, there are now more households with two or more earners. So it has become harder for many households to choose housing that minimizes commuting journeys for all their workers, since the jobs may be quite far apart. High job turnover rates also make it difficult for households to maintain short commuting distances. Taking a new job may replace an initially short commute with a much longer one. In some industries, movement among jobs occurs at high rates. These factors can both cause and perpetuate jobs-housing imbalances.[9]

EXCLUSIONARY PRACTICES BY LOCAL GOVERNMENTS. Many communities near large outlying job clusters appear to have deliberately adopted local ordinances that drive up housing prices. Hence, many people who work in communities with high housing costs cannot afford to live there and must commute long distances to housing they can afford.

Some local governments engage in tactics of raising the cost of housing to improve their fiscal health. Most believe that commercial real estate uses—which entail jobs—produce local tax expenditure gains, whereas low- and moderate-income residents cause net tax expenditure losses. So such governments adopt zoning and other ordinances that encourage commercial land uses and discourage relatively modest-cost housing. These policies stimulate more local jobs than housing units, thereby contributing to a *quantitative* jobs-housing imbalance. Such policies also create a *qualitative* imbalance by preventing local construction of housing affordable to many local workers. Such exclusionary policies include growth moratoriums, downzoning to prohibit even moderate-density housing, restriction of land zoned for multifamily housing, long delays in review and approval of permits, and costly reporting and environmental protection requirements.

Tactics for Changing Existing Imbalances

Reducing existing jobs-housing imbalances within a metropolitan area has often been proposed as a means of cutting traffic congestion. There are five possible ways to achieve a closer jobs-housing balance in each of the various types of imbalanced areas described above:

1. Add large numbers of new housing units in or near areas with a job surplus by increasing the total quantity of units built there; and

changing the quality of new housing built there by creating more housing units suitable for occupancy by low- and moderate-wage workers employed there.

2. Block the creation of many more jobs in areas with a job surplus.

3. Move existing jobs from areas with a job surplus to newer areas with a housing surplus.

4. Encourage the formation of most jobs in areas with a housing surplus rather than in those with a job surplus.

5. Inhibit the creation of additional housing units in newer areas with a housing surplus.

These tactics are closely related and several must be carried out simultaneously to create a more balanced jobs-housing situation in an entire metropolitan area. If some are successfully implemented but others are not, the overall housing situation could become worse. For example, if building more housing units in areas with a housing surplus was successfully slowed but no more relatively low-priced units were created in areas with a job surplus, the shortage of affordable housing would increase. If population growth nevertheless continued, the result would be a doubling-up of low-income households in units built for single-family occupancy. This occurred in much of Southern California during the 1980s.

Thus, successfully improving the jobs-housing balance throughout a metropolitan area requires complex coordination of very different policies in its different subregions. But in nearly all U.S. metropolitan areas, control over key land-use policies is divided among dozens or even hundreds of local governments with parochial perspectives. This fragmented structure poses enormous obstacles to carrying out the type of cohesive, integrated strategy necessary to achieve an areawide jobs-housing balance.

Feasibility of Tactics for Changing Balances

Several factors will influence the feasibility of public policies aimed at improving jobs-housing balances.

WORKERS' PREFERENCES. Most policies seeking to reduce jobs-housing imbalances implicitly assume that most people would like to live as close to their jobs as possible, but experience suggests otherwise, particularly that of people living in large master-planned communities. These communities have been developed to contain both jobs and housing affordable to the people that hold those jobs. More-over, the housing is conveniently accessible to the jobs by car, foot, bicycle, and bus. Yet a study of fifteen matched pairs of both planned and unplanned communities showed no significant difference in the work and commuting behavior of their residents.[10] In both types, more than 84 percent of residents chose to work at some distance from their homes; the average commuting time was twenty-five minutes; the average distance was from 9.9 to 10.8 miles; and the shares of workers commuting different distances were similar.

Moreover, in a survey of twenty-two San Francisco Bay area com-munities, a majority of workers living in most communities were employed elsewhere (the average was 63 percent); and a majority working there lived elsewhere (that average was 62 percent).[11] This strong pattern of cross-commuting surely indicates that where work-ers choose to live is influenced by many factors other than the length of their commuting journeys.

Thus, making nearby housing in appropriate price ranges available to workers employed in a job center will not persuade most of them to live there. A great many factors enter into people's residential choices, including where their relatives and friends live, the quality of life in different neighborhoods, the quality of local schools, where jobs of others members of the household are located, and the age, ethnic composition, and socioeconomic status of the local population. Neighborhoods containing a tremendous variety of these traits are found in most metropolitan areas. That is why so many people choose to live far from their jobs—even when they can find housing they could afford much closer to those jobs.

CHOOSING APPROPRIATE GEOGRAPHIC SUBREGIONS. Bal-ancing jobs and housing must be related to specific subregions in a metropolitan area. Within each subregion, the number and types of jobs are supposed to match the number and types of housing units. Hence, an essential part of any balancing strategy is to decide exactly where to draw subregional boundaries.

In theory, such boundaries ought to demarcate so-called commute sheds; that is, areas considered to be within desirable commuting range of major job centers. However, putting this concept into practice is extremely difficult:

There are often multiple important employment centers (and, therefore, multiple arguable focal points for overlapping commute sheds)
within a given subarea of Southern California. And, since most
households now involve more than one wage earner, and each
wage earner may be involved in an occupation whose practitioners
need to be concentrated in a different employment center, a single
household may fall within two or more commute sheds separated
by 20 miles or more. Because most commute sheds cross municipal
lines, and often many of them, there is usually no local government . . . jurisdictionally competent to set or carry out jobs-housing balance policy for the full shed. Finally . . . most municipalities
in Los Angeles County contain the workplaces of only a tiny fraction
of their residents.[12]

The smaller the share of a total metropolitan area encompassed
within any subregion, the more likely that subregion is to contain a
disproportionate fraction of either jobs or housing compared with the
area as a whole—and therefore the more likely it is to be imbalanced.
This means the entire balancing act is greatly affected by a purely
arbitrary decision concerning how large the subregions are made.
Moreover, size is not the only vital dimension involved. As politicians
in charge of electoral districting have long known, there are myriad
ways to draw boundaries for subregions of equal population or area
within some larger territory. Yet the feasibility of achieving a desired
jobs-housing balance depends on exactly how boundaries are drawn
for the subregions concerned.

Most subregions will be created by combining smaller communities
that already have legally defined boundaries. This makes it easier to
collect data and is more acceptable politically than creating wholly
new entities. But the people deciding how to define subregions will
be tempted to choose boundaries that minimize the difficulties of
attaining whatever definition of balance they are using. Thus the
definition of subregions will inevitably become semipolitical, rather
than purely technical or scientific.

ACHIEVING A QUALITATIVE JOBS-HOUSING BALANCE
WITHIN EACH SUBREGION. As noted above, having enough ap-
propriate-quality housing units within each subregion to shelter the

number of workers employed there is not sufficient to attain a jobs-housing balance. For one thing, the average distance between the housing units and the jobs within each such subregion would have to be shorter than current average suburban commuting distances. That would only be possible if each subregion were small. But the smaller each subregion, the more difficult it is to attain an appropriate balance therein.

Furthermore, even if the number of jobs and housing units within each small subregion were perfectly balanced quantitatively, they would most likely remain imbalanced qualitatively. Thus, thousands of new units could be built in Santa Clara County, California, near Silicon Valley, to offset the large surplus of jobs there. But the cost of housing units there averaged more than $240,000 in 1990.[13] If most new units added had similar prices, many workers employed there could not afford them. Experience proves that "natural" forces will not appropriately match local housing prices to the wage levels of locally employed workers within each subregion because local government policies raise housing prices in many communities. The policies necessary to overcome such local regulatory barriers to affordable housing are complex and difficult both to get adopted and to implement.[14]

THE ADMINISTRATIVE DIFFICULTIES OF ACHIEVING A JOBS-HOUSING BALANCE. A jobs-housing strategy would require creating a regional agency with strong authority over local government land-use policies. Only such a regional agency could coherently (1) choose the specific boundaries of the subregions within which balancing should occur, (2) determine which communities could use more jobs and housing and where additional jobs and housing should be discouraged, (3) pass regulations aimed at achieving those goals, and (4) monitor the subsequent behavior of the communities involved. But a regional agency that powerful has at least two serious drawbacks. First, this approach would entail transferring considerable sovereignty over land-use decisions from local governments to a regional agency. Such a power shift is sure to encounter vehement and sustained opposition from most local governments and citizens. Second, such a powerful regional agency would form another layer of government regulation affecting the real estate development process. That process is already burdened with lengthy delays that greatly increase development costs. These difficulties are explored further in chapter 10.

THE POLICY TIME-LAG PROBLEM. Another problem is likely to arise from the inherent dynamism of job and housing markets. When the regional agency mandated to seek greater jobs-housing balance is established, it will set targets for each subregion on the basis of data already several years old, because of the difficulties of obtaining current information. By the time its policies become even partly implemented, at least several more years will have passed. By then, many of the overall and individual adjustments to long commuting journeys described earlier will have taken place. That will make the actual relationship between jobs and housing in every community quite different from what the regional agency first thought it would be. Hence the policies may no longer be appropriate.

Such policy obsolescence because of informational and implementation time lags is endemic to many government actions in a dynamic society. It is particularly likely to plague any strategy to attain a jobs-housing balance because of the high mobility of American households. In 1987, 8.5 percent of owner-occupant households and 37.5 percent of renter-occupants had moved within the previous twelve months. The fraction moving annually was 21 percent higher in the West than in the rest of the nation. Thus, even if an appropriate jobs-housing balance is attained at some moment, it will be difficult to sustain.[15]

"SPONTANEOUS" ACHIEVEMENT OF TACTICS. Recently major U.S. metropolitan areas have been "spontaneously" implementing some of the tactics listed above without any explicit public policies aimed at doing so. For example, more housing has been added to older, more central areas with a job surplus. But in most metropolitan areas, these additions have been much smaller than the number of jobs added through new downtown office space occupancy. Really significant housing increases in close-in neighborhoods require raising density, which has encountered severe political opposition. Hence the first tactic listed earlier has not been taken up on any large scale.

In contrast, for the past thirty years there has been a major and nearly universal outmigration of both jobs and residents from central cities to suburbs. This has accomplished the second, third, and fourth tactics listed above to some degree. It has caused some spontaneous improvement in the jobs-housing balance in areas with a job surplus and those with a housing surplus. Jobs are likely to continue moving into outlying areas with housing surpluses, probably at an accelerating rate. But a lot of new housing has also been built in these peripheral areas, and this trend is likely to continue unless deliberately opposed. Up to now, such new homebuilding has more than offset the movement of additional jobs into these areas.[16] Hence most such areas still have large housing surpluses.

Moreover, during the 1980s, many additional jobs were created in downtown areas because so much new office space was built there. This directly contravened the second tactic set forth above, and indirectly opposed the third and fourth tactics. In general, then, recent trends are probably worsening the jobs-housing imbalances in most U.S. metropolitan areas.[17]

The Political Asymmetry Problem

A great difficulty in trying to improve subregional jobs-housing balances through public policies is that the five tactics described earlier will meet with varying political responses. Some are almost sure to be rejected, whereas others are quite likely to be adopted. This would cause incomplete and distorted application of the complete set of policies. The net result might increase rather than decrease commuting problems.

The tactics most likely to be rejected are those connected with building more housing for low- and moderate-income households in or near areas with a job surplus. Such areas include downtowns and large outlying nodes containing retail, office, and industrial facilities. Since most such areas contain few vacant parcels, many additional housing units could only be built there if existing structures were razed and the area redeveloped at higher densities. But present residents would strongly resist higher densities.

Local governments would also resist limits on adding more jobs. They want the added local tax revenues such jobs provide. As a result, two key ingredients of any overall jobs-housing balancing strategy would be extremely difficult to put in place politically.

Other subregions suffer from the opposite problem: a surplus of housing units in relation to jobs. There the appropriate balancing policy would be to inhibit more housing construction. That policy would probably be enthusiastically accepted by many existing residents and local governments eager to limit further growth. Hence many such communities would adopt growth limits reducing annual additions to the housing supply. But those communities are also the ones in which the least expensive new housing in each metropolitan area is being built. Consequently, the policies that are supposed to improve the balance between jobs and housing might choke off the creation of additional new, relatively low-cost housing in peripheral areas—without adding many new units in older areas with job surpluses. This outcome would make the shortage of affordable housing worse and would not shorten average commuting distances.[18]

The Jobs-Housing Balance and Traffic Congestion

Even if the jobs-housing balances within a metropolitan area were improved, how much would that cut traffic congestion? The direct goal of such changes would be to decrease average commuting distance. As discussed in chapter 6, that would not necessarily reduce traffic congestion; other conditions are also required. However, the main issue is, would improving the jobs-housing balance significantly reduce average commuting distances?

To answer that question, one must first specify just what is meant by "improving the jobs-housing balance." Public policy cannot and should not dictate to every worker where he or she must live so as to reduce traffic congestion. Therefore, what could public policies concerning the jobs-housing balance be expected to achieve? The answer is the creation of enough housing near each major job center, at appropriate price levels, so that every worker in that center could *in theory* live within a relatively short commuting distance.

Since most workers do not choose their housing solely to minimize their commuting times, however, even if an adequate supply of appropriately priced housing were created near every job center, many workers in each center would not occupy that housing. Large amounts of cross-commuting would still take place. But would there be much less cross-commuting than there is now? No one knows, nor has much research been done on this subject. Workers employed in large job centers in Southern California had longer commutes than those employed outside such centers, except for centers located in exurban parts of the metropolitan area.[19] Data from the 1980 census also indicate that the shortest commuting times were among workers who lived and worked outside the central cities. The longest were among those who lived outside central cities but worked downtown.[20] So if many jobs were moved out of the large clusters where they now outnumber nearby housing units, or many new housing units were built near them, the average commuting distances should decline.

The maximum possible reduction in average commuting distances from an improved jobs-housing balance can be estimated from the model metropolitan area set forth in appendix C. In that model, workers both reside and work in three subregions: the central city, older suburbs, and newer exurbs. In the base case, one-third of the population lives in the central city, one-half in the older suburbs, and one-sixth in the exurbs. But 40 percent of the jobs are in the central city, 55 percent in the suburbs, and only 5 percent in the exurbs. The ratio of local jobs to locally resident workers is 0.29 for the exurbs, 1.10 for the older suburbs, and 1.20 for the central city; so substantial imbalances exit. About 42 percent of all workers commute from one subregion to another. The average commuting distance for all workers is 11.4 miles.

Job locations can be adjusted to cut cross-commuting among subregions in half, so that only 21 percent of all workers are cross-commuting. Then the ratio of local jobs to locally resident workers is 0.65 for the exurbs, 1.05 for the older suburbs, and 1.10 for the central city. All subregions are closer to being balanced. The average commuting distance is 9.59 miles, or 15.8 percent less than in the base case. That is a considerable reduction in average commuting distances. If the proportion of cross-commuting is reduced by 25 percent instead of 50 percent, the average commuting distance for all metropolitan area workers declines by 8.9 percent, to 10.39 miles.

These simulations do not take into account the immense real-world obstacles to actually shifting that many jobs. Nor do they include movements of housing locations. Moreover, reducing average commuting distances does not always alleviate traffic congestion. However, actual declines in average commuting distances of the magnitude derived from the model would probably improve traffic congestion significantly, other things being equal.

In summary, a jobs-housing balancing strategy is not likely to reduce traffic congestion effectively, even in the long run, for three main reasons. First, deliberately decreasing existing jobs-housing imbalances throughout any large U.S. metropolitan area is extraordinarily difficult. The range of policies required, the depth of institutional change needed, and the extremely strong political resistance that must be overcome are all immense. It is a task akin to moving mountains without using either bulldozers or dynamite. Within the fragmented institutional structure of U.S. metropolitan areas, doing so verges on the impossible.

Second, the resulting improvements in traffic congestion are probably not large, and would be difficult to sustain. Matching the affordable housing supply in an area with the wage earners who work there would not necessarily persuade the latter to occupy the former. Even if policymakers achieved such a match, many locally employed workers would still choose to live far from their jobs to gain other benefits besides minimizing their commutes.

The final argument against this strategy is that the energy and degree of institutional change it requires would cut traffic congestion much more if used to implement other strategies aimed at the same goal. Examples are adopting peak-hour road pricing or peak-hour parking charges. Such major institutional changes can be achieved only through expenditure of strong personal leadership and energy, plus accumulated political capital. Why focus those scarce resources on altering an area's jobs-housing imbalances when other institutional changes would be much more effective at cutting traffic congestion?

This does not mean that improving the jobs-housing balance in a region is a bad idea or that it would produce no social benefits. If accomplished, it could help provide greater justice and equality of housing and job opportunities for low- and moderate-income households, improve the availability of the local labor force in suburban communities, increase socioeconomic and cultural diversity in such communities, and enable both old and young members of families living there to remain residents of those communities. Hence it may be socially desirable to try improving the jobs-housing balances in many communities or even throughout a metropolitan area, but that strategy should not be pursued primarily to reduce traffic congestion.

Eight

Concentrating Jobs
in Large Clusters

S OME ADVOCATES of the greater use of public transit to relieve traffic congestion and air pollution propose concentrating more jobs in large clusters outside of downtowns. By providing
common commuting destinations for larger numbers of workers, this
would encourage greater commuting via transit and ride sharing.
This chapter examines how practical this strategy might be in U.S.
metropolitan areas.

Advantages of Job Concentration

The basic economics of mass transit for commuting require that its
riders share either a common origin or a common destination or both.
That would happen if many jobs were concentrated within a small
area. Then enough workers could ride the same transit vehicles to pay
for the operation of those vehicles, which are far costlier to buy and
run than private automobiles. If a much larger fraction of all workers
commuted by mass transit, then the total number of vehicles on the
roads would decline enough to reduce peak-hour congestion. That is
one justification for a job-concentration strategy.

Large job centers thus formed might be linked by fixed-rail mass
transit, as in many European metropolitan areas. That arrangement is
clearly most feasible in areas that already have extensive mass transit
systems. An optimal system would permit workers located in any part
of the metropolitan area to commute to any job center with no more
than one transfer. But even areas without fixed-rail systems could
connect major job concentrations with buses operating on exclusive
busways or in HOV lanes.

A job-concentration strategy has recently been proposed for the greater Toronto area that would bring many jobs together in a few big clusters.[1] This "nodal" strategy would presumably reduce the need for automobile commuting and encourage greater use of public transportation. It is visualized as lying somewhere between two other strategies also proposed: the "spread" strategy, which promotes continued low-density sprawl supported by massive new freeway construction; and the "central" strategy, which concentrates most future population and job growth within the inner parts of the metropolitan area, relies heavily on public transit, and calls for only minimal freeway expansion. As of late 1991, no decision had yet been made about which of these strategies—if any—Toronto's public policy will follow.

The other reason for adopting a job-concentration strategy is similar but involves ride sharing. Since many workers will have the same points of departure and commuting destinations, more will find it easier to share rides in their own cars or in vans provided by their employers. Also, clustering many firms together makes it easier to create strong transportation management associations (TMAs) through which employers can jointly urge workers to share rides. Experience shows that ride sharing increases dramatically when employers put great pressure on their workers to use it and reward those who do.

Job concentrations also allow TMAs to provide certain direct services for workers more efficiently than if the firms involved were scattered widely. For example, TMAs can provide shuttle buses or shuttle vans linking different parts of the job-concentration area for a low fee or even free. This would make it easier for employees to visit one another, lunch together, or shop during lunch breaks without using their cars, thereby reducing local congestion.

Once employers in a cluster started working together to promote ride sharing, they could more easily undertake other tactics for reducing congestion. For example, they might stagger their work hours. They could also agree not to provide free parking to their employees. They could do that without becoming noncompetitive with employers at other locations by providing commuting allowances to all their workers and by charging those who drove alone for parking spaces.

If large job concentrations could feasibly be created within either suburbs or large cities, there is little doubt that they could more easily generate additional ride sharing, and perhaps more use of mass transit than now occurs. This strategy would not reduce average commuting distances unless the housing locations of workers also changed. Moreover, job concentration is somewhat in conflict with achieving a better jobs-housing balance. In theory, the latter would be better served by scattering jobs widely, closer to housing.

Feasibility of Job Concentration

In assessing this strategy for U.S. metropolitan areas, several factors should be taken into account.

1. Existing jobs are now widely scattered, especially in suburban communities, with the result that concentrating significant fractions of them in big centers would require major relocations. Job dispersal has been encouraged by suburban zoning ordinances that prohibit high-density commercial construction. These regulations mandate low-rise, well-landscaped workplaces served by their own parking lots, or they locate businesses in elongated ribbons along major commercial streets. This pattern is strikingly illustrated by 1980 data from the five-county Los Angeles area for nineteen large activity centers covering 23,980 acres and containing 821,700 jobs. The biggest was the downtown Los Angeles core, which held 373,300 jobs in 6,737 acres. But all nineteen centers combined accounted for only 17.5 percent of the 4.7 million jobs in the five-county area. The remaining 82.5 percent were scattered outside these centers. Thus job concentration in the Los Angeles area is best described as dispersed rather than polycentric.[2] Comparable breakdowns of employment data are not readily available for most other large U.S. metropolitan areas. Yet it seems quite likely that at least a majority of jobs are more or less dispersed in nearly all of them.

As a result, concentrating much greater fractions of existing jobs in activity centers would require a massive relocation of existing employers. This strategy can be much more effectively applied to the initial settlement of areas of new growth than to the rearrangement of areas already settled. It would have to be adopted by planners and governments of areas of new growth before those areas were settled and used to influence where future jobs were located therein.

2. Each large metropolitan area already contains several major outlying employment centers, but most people who work there do not commute by public transit. Most such centers are clusters of employers

around regional shopping malls. Examples are Tyson's Corner outside of Washington, D.C., Oakbrook outside of Chicago, the South Coast Plaza in Orange County, California, and the Galleria in Houston. These "edge cities" contain thousands of jobs in retail, office, service, light industrial, and warehouse structures.[3]

However, these structures are not right next to each other, as are downtown buildings. Rather, each building is surrounded by its own parking lots, which isolate it from other structures. This makes pedestrian movement both aesthetically unattractive and inefficient and encourages the use of cars both to commute and to move between buildings. Higher fractions of workers commute by automotive vehicles to these outlying centers than to downtowns, which are better served by transit. The 1980 data on the Los Angeles area cited above showed that only 8.3 percent of workers in the eighteen largest activity centers outside of the downtown commuted by public transit, compared with 20.7 percent of downtown workers and 3.5 percent of all workers not employed in any of the nineteen largest centers. Therefore, outlying centers generate more automotive traffic per 1,000 workers than downtowns—especially around noontime. This often gives rise to three rush hours, rather than just those in the morning and evening.

Thus, the mere existence of large job concentrations does not create conditions conducive to greater transit commuting. The concentrations must be compact enough so that most workers can easily walk to one or a few transit stops, and transit service must be frequent. Both conditions are rare in existing outlying activity centers.

3. Most suburban communities would oppose concentrating jobs in just a few large centers because they seek to capture as many jobs as they can within their boundaries to maximize local tax revenues. The fragmented structure of local governments in most U.S. metropolitan areas causes intense competition for commercial "ratables." Large job concentrations would undoubtedly be located in a relatively small fraction of all the local communities within a metropolitan area. The only exception would be areas such as the one around Washington, D.C., where entire counties make up the main local governments. The few communities containing large job concentrations would benefit greatly from the tax revenues generated there. But surrounding communities would suffer from having lower tax bases and would try to prevent jobs from moving into these few centers by offering employers

more advantageous tax and benefit packages. Therefore, in most metropolitan areas, local governments would be more likely to oppose a
job-concentration strategy—unless some new method of funding local
governments were adopted.

4. This strategy would not by itself reduce traffic congestion; it
would have to be accompanied by substantial changes in transportation arrangements. Most workers in large suburban job centers drive
to work alone. Concentrating many jobs in a few big centers would
initially increase congestion there because so many more auto-driving
commuters would converge on them each day, which means that
the job-concentration strategy can decrease congestion only if it is
accompanied by one or both of two other actions. One is the provision
of greatly expanded and improved public transit facilities and service.
The other is the vigorous promotion of private ride-sharing programs
by key private and public employers there. Prospects for those tactics
were discussed in chapter 5.

5. Getting any sizable fraction of U.S. workers—especially those
living in suburbs—to commute by public transit would require extensive changes in their behavior that they now strongly resist. The
proportion of suburban-resident workers who commuted by private
vehicles was 90.8 percent in 1977 and 89.1 percent in 1983.[4] The
proportion using public transit fell slightly, from 4.6 percent in 1977
to 3.3 percent in 1983. There is no evidence that concentrating jobs in
big suburban clusters would produce any notable changes in commuting behavior. Surveys in Walnut Creek, California, concerning how
workers commute to offices in large job clusters next to fixed-rail mass
transit stops indicate that *less* than 2 percent use mass transit.[5]

6. Fixed-rail public transit systems are costly to build, and almost all
public transit systems—including buses—incur large operating losses.
Even if this strategy succeeded in changing commuter behavior, it
would impose heavy financial burdens on governments. Most public
transit systems throughout the world lose money on both their construction costs and current operations.[6] Raising fares on fixed-rail
systems to cover their full costs is either politically unacceptable or
would reduce their patronage to unfeasibly low levels, or both. Consequently, few metropolitan areas anywhere will build fixed-rail transit
systems without substantial subsidies from their national governments. Also, extensive public transit systems can only rarely be operated without large ongoing subsidies. Because the job-concentration

strategy requires greater use of public transit to reduce congestion, it would need massive subsidies not now available.

7. If job concentration led to the development of an effective ride sharing program, it could reduce traffic congestion to some extent without undue public expense. Employers could more easily cooperate to promote ride sharing among their workers if clustered in a sizable activity center than if widely scattered. Moreover, many more workers would have access to a bigger group of possible riders from which to form car or van pools. Ride sharing can be carried out without much public expense. It would be even further encouraged by the creation of HOV lanes on nearby expressways, although that would involve heavy public expenditures. Furthermore, once employer associations were formed to promote ride sharing, they could more effectively implement other tactics aimed at reducing traffic congestion, as noted earlier.

Administrative Problems in Implementing Job Concentration

Concentrating most new suburban jobs within a few outlying centers would require two institutional changes in most U.S. metropolitan areas. One would permit many communities to share in the tax revenues generated by those centers. The only nonconsolidated U.S. metropolitan area that now has such an arrangement is Minnesota's Twin Cities area, which uses tax-base sharing. The second institutional change would give a regional agency the power to encourage job concentration, perhaps by prohibiting added jobs in certain areas. Otherwise, competition among individual communities would continue the broad scattering of jobs.

Thus a job-concentration strategy would require regulatory intervention into current land-use decisionmaking. It would probably create another layer of regulation that would control, or at least strongly influence, where potential employers could locate their jobs. Many employers, except perhaps the smallest, might have to obtain permission from a regional job control agency when deciding where to locate or expand. This would be a radical departure from the universal and traditional U.S. practice of permitting individual employers to enjoy the freedom of locational choice. The whole idea would surely be repugnant to nearly all U.S. employers and local governments.[7]

The only alternative would be some market-oriented incentive structure that motivated individual employers to locate in key job centers and avoid other sites. For example, property tax rates could be made much lower in such centers and higher elsewhere (but most firms do not base their locational decisions primarily on property taxes). Or a special worker surtax might be imposed on all firms that newly locate outside selected job centers, but not on those that move inside those centers. This would at least leave locational decisions up to individual employers. But it would require discriminatory taxes or fees that might be found illegal. Such incentives would still require a powerful role by either a regional or state agency. Only such an agency could decide which parts of the metropolitan area would be favored with positive inducements and which would suffer from negative ones.

Furthermore, a job-concentration strategy would confer a quasi-monopoly position on the owners of land within the selected job clusters. Unless there were so many designated job centers that competition among them restrained land prices in all of them, they would be able to charge exorbitantly high prices or rents for their land. This could only be avoided through commercial rent controls or land-price controls, or by government acquisition and administration of all the land within the job-concentration zones. Neither is compatible with normal free-enterprise behavior. Conversely, a job-concentration policy would deprive many owners of land outside the selected centers of all chances to gain high property values or rents from commercial land uses. Those landowners would fiercely oppose this strategy, and they would vastly outnumber landowners benefited by it. This stacks the deck politically against the adoption of such a scheme in a democracy.

In fact, this situation illustrates a general difficulty with policies designed to curb purely individualistic behavior in order to achieve community goals. There is an inescapable conflict between unconstrained individual freedoms long traditional among Americans and certain widely desired community objectives they now seek. As noted earlier, this conflict is inherent in many policies aimed at reducing traffic congestion.

Where a Job-Concentration Strategy Might Work

There is one type of U.S. metropolitan area in which a job-concentration strategy might feasibly help reduce future traffic congestion.

A few metropolitan areas are dominated by geographically large local governments, such as the county governments around Washington, D.C. These governments encompass huge territories that already contain major job centers. So they could steer at least some additional jobs into those few centers without creating another layer of government, particularly by pressuring owners of currently developed sites in such centers to fill in those sites with more structures. New commercial buildings could be placed in present parking or landscaped areas, and more parking could be provided by decking other parking lots. This would convert now sprawling but inefficient offices in these centers into more compact, downtown-like districts, would permit more efficient pedestrian interchanges, and would encourage more ride sharing, and—if these centers were served by rapid transit—more commuting off the highways.

Since these governments already contain both the areas that would lose potential jobs under such a policy and the centers that would gain jobs, they would not have to adopt new tax-sharing arrangements. And they could use their existing development permission powers to steer new jobs into these centers, thereby avoiding two serious obstacles to the job-concentration strategy.

Can an Effective Job-Concentration Strategy Be Achieved?

All the above factors indicate that a deliberate strategy of suburban job concentration is not likely to play a significant role in reducing future traffic congestion in U.S. metropolitan areas. One reason is that it would force long-established worker and employer behavior patterns to change. However, that is true of almost any strategy likely to reduce future traffic congestion.

More important, in a world of fragmented local governments, a job-concentration strategy would require regional bureaucratic control over job locations. That would add another layer to the already complex real estate development process. Moreover, the fiscal system that now finances most local governments would have to be greatly modified so that those communities containing big job clusters would not capture unfair shares of property tax revenue. The required legal and institutional changes would be extremely unpopular among both local governments and employers. And one result would be increased monopoly power over land prices by those fortunate enough to own property within the chosen concentration areas.

Furthermore, for maximum effectiveness, this strategy must be linked to extensive public transit facilities. Metropolitan areas that already have fixed-rail systems could tie additional job centers into those systems, or just expand the job centers they now contain. But most U.S. metropolitan areas do not have off-road mass transit systems and would require huge public investments in building them to link job centers. This would be necessary even to serve such centers only with bus transit. Buses would need exclusive busways or HOV lanes for maximum effectiveness. And all additional transit facilities would require continuous subsidies to help pay for their operating costs. Such added spending is not likely to be forthcoming from governments at any level.

Nevertheless, metropolitan areas with four specific traits might at least consider adopting some elements of a job-concentration strategy. They should (1) have more than 1.2 million residents, (2) suffer from severe traffic congestion, (3) contain a few, geographically large suburban governments, and (4) already have fixed-rail mass transit systems. Because of their large suburban political jurisdictions, they could avoid some of the most controversial intergovernmental power struggles that would otherwise accompany this strategy. But smaller metropolitan areas, or those with highly fragmented local government structures, or those without extensive existing public transit systems are not likely to find this strategy very effective. The latter group includes the vast majority of U.S. metropolitan areas.

Nine

Local Growth-Management Policies

MANY LOCAL governments have reacted to rising traffic congestion by adopting ordinances that limit future development within their boundaries. This chapter examines the nature and impact of such ordinances, and their likely effectiveness in reducing congestion.[1]

Why Local Governments Adopt Growth Controls to Reduce Traffic Congestion

Local growth-management laws can focus on commercial development, residential development, or both. At least forty-one types of such policies have been identified in past studies.[2] These include caps on the number of housing units or square feet of commercial space that can be built annually, height limits on commercial buildings, downzoning of vacant parcels to reduce the density at which they can be developed, and many others. This book cannot go into the details of such policies, but it assumes the policies would decrease the amount of future growth in the adopting community. But how effective could growth-management policies be in reducing traffic congestion?

In theory, since traffic flows are generated by commercial and residential developments, decreasing the future amount of such development within the community will reduce the traffic flows arising there. Local governments have often used this argument to restrict commercial development and multifamily housing projects. For example, Walnut Creek, California, in response to increasing traffic congestion in its downtown area, prohibited office developments above a certain height and building size.

Other relevant growth-management policies force developers to bear some of the costs of the roads necessary to handle traffic generated by their projects. This can be done through impact fees or exactions required before awarding permission to build new projects. Or a community may adopt some form of "concurrence" policy. That means it will not grant permission for new developments until the infrastructures needed to serve them are either already built or at least planned and paid for. Florida has adopted such a policy statewide.

In the late 1980s, local growth-management policies became a widespread local government response to rising traffic congestion. In California in particular, hundreds of communities adopted such laws, ostensibly to combat traffic congestion.[3] Three factors in particular influenced these decisions.

First, traffic congestion was growing much worse, and local politicians and government leaders wanted to appear to be doing something in response. Since the basic causes of congestion are regionwide in nature, not local, local leaders cannot directly control the true causes of congestion unless they carry out highly controversial policies throughout the region. Not only would that daunting task take years, but it would also run counter to their strong desire to preserve their own local sovereignty. Second, local officials can readily pass purely local ordinances, often without much controversy. Hence they do so in order to appear responsive to their constituents' concerns about this problem. Such laws need not be entirely symbolic, although they usually do not affect many fundamental causes of congestion.

Third, most social costs imposed by local growth-management laws are not borne mainly by existing residents within the adopting communities, but by potential future residents and people living elsewhere. The largest such cost is higher future housing prices faced by persons seeking to move into the community. But those higher housing prices also benefit existing homeowners, who usually account for a majority of the local electorate. Hence there is a strong political incentive for local officials to adopt such policies.

Can Local Growth Controls Affect Traffic Congestion?

In reality, locally adopted growth-management policies can have little, if any, impact on existing traffic congestion levels within the communities that pass them. Almost all new local growth-management policies regulate future growth. But today's traffic is generated by past growth that is already in place.

Whether a community's policies can affect its future traffic congestion levels depends on three main factors. The first is whether most of its traffic is generated locally or somewhere else. If locally, then local ordinances may be able to keep future traffic flows from rising as much as they would if growth proceeded unchecked. But if most local traffic arises elsewhere and passes through the adopting community, its laws may not affect its future traffic flows at all. Then the key factor is how much additional future development will occur where most of its traffic is being generated, which is presumably beyond its control.

The second key factor is whether the adopting community contains much available land on which developers could build more traffic-generating uses. Such land could be vacant sites or sites improved with structures that could be replaced by or renovated into higher-intensity uses. If the community contains little such land, its future growth will be limited, regardless of the policies it adopts. Hence growth-management policies would not greatly affect its future traffic flows. However, communities with very little developable land are not likely to adopt such policies.

The third important factor to consider is to what extent the growth diverted from the adopting community by its growth-management policies will relocate to areas where it still generates traffic passing through that community. As noted in chapter 2, no one suburb can influence the overall growth of its entire metropolitan area by adopting local growth-management policies. At most, such policies will simply shift growth from the adopting community to others nearby. Some of the added traffic generated by this diverted growth may still pass through the adopting community. Since the growth diverted away from any one community is likely to spread over many others, it is highly improbable that all the traffic generated by this displaced growth will still flow through the community from which it was diverted.

All three of these conditions are most likely to prevail in new-growth suburbs on the edges of metropolitan areas. Those suburbs not only contain the largest amounts of vacant land, but also have the fewest other communities lying beyond them that might generate traffic flowing back through them. These three conditions are necessary but not sufficient to ensure that local ordinances will actually influence the community's future traffic congestion. Whether that happens depends on the specific policies adopted.

The Direct Effect on Local Land Uses

Local growth-management policies can affect local land use in at least four ways. They can influence the specific uses carried out on particular sites. This is done by prohibiting certain uses that developers would otherwise pursue because of their high profitability, such as multifamily housing in neighborhoods occupied primarily by single-family homes. Such policies can also limit annual additions to the local supply of property, for example, by putting a cap on the number of additional housing units that developers are allowed to build each year. They can raise private development costs by (1) adding directly to costs, (2) increasing the amount of time required to complete any project, or (3) reducing the density of development permitted on a given site. And they can increase public sector costs by requiring construction of certain public improvements before private development is permitted.

Effects on the Community and Its Metropolitan Area

Growth-management policies also affect the community adopting them and its metropolitan area. To begin with, they slow the pace of new development within the adopting locality. That is the main purpose of most local growth-management policies.

Also, nearly all such policies raise the market prices of both new and existing housing and other properties within the adopting community by restricting supplies there. This also causes higher rents because land values increase and rental units are in scarcer supply than they would otherwise be. Most empirical studies indicate a housing price increase in the adopting community of 5–10 percent, although one study showed a 17–38 percent increase.[4]

Higher housing prices and rents make the adopting community more socially exclusionary by shifting its composition to a higher-income group than it would otherwise have had. However, this change takes a long time, unless the community's total population is growing rapidly. If many communities within a metropolitan area adopt growth-management policies, low- and moderate-income households will find it harder to become homeowners, or even to find rental accommodations they can afford.

But higher housing prices also increase the wealth of the community's existing homeowners, who usually form a majority of its households. This positive effect generates strong political support for such policies. It also means that higher housing prices in themselves cannot be judged a priori as harmful to society, even though they make it harder for low- and moderate-income households to become homeowners.[5] However, the losers from higher home prices are generally poorer than the gainers. So the widespread adoption of growth-management policies has a regressive net impact on the distribution of incomes and wealth in the general metropolitan area.

Local growth-management policies may have yet another effect: some increase the demand for housing within the adopting communities. When a community adopts exclusionary policies, the price of homes there may initially rise because of smaller additions to supply. Higher prices would normally reduce the demand for housing there. But if many households within the metropolitan area value exclusivity for its own sake, the community's increased exclusivity may increase demand for housing there, in spite of the higher prices.[6] That would drive housing prices there still higher, with all the effects described above.

In addition, growth-management policies tend to spread the ultimate growth of the metropolitan area over a larger space than it would otherwise have occupied. Such policies generally reduce the fully built-out density of the communities that adopt them, compared with what those densities would have been. Therefore, the more communities adopt such policies, the lower the average density of the metropolitan area, and the larger the territory its built-up areas must occupy to accommodate any given total population.

Effects on Traffic Congestion

By slowing the pace of new development within the communities that adopt them, local growth controls can reduce future increases in locally generated traffic—if these communities have the three traits mentioned earlier.

If such policies force developers to build or pay for more roads and other traffic-handling facilities than would otherwise have been built, they may increase the traffic-handling capacity of the locality's road system. This could also reduce future traffic congestion there. However, developers are generally required to build intersections, exit and entry lanes, parking areas, and other spot traffic-handling facilities, rather than add to the general capacity of the community's road system.

By diverting future growth to other communities, growth- management policies shift future traffic there, too. Finally, by spreading future development of the entire metropolitan area during any given period over a larger territory than it would otherwise have occupied, growth-management policies require households to drive longer distances. That adds to the metropolitan area's total traffic flows, probably increasing future traffic congestion.

In sum, growth management laws can reduce future peak-hour traffic congestion within the communities passing them under some circumstances. But they do so only at the expense of increasing future congestion within the rest of their metropolitan areas. Hence they can hardly be considered desirable from the viewpoint of society as a whole. Although the congestion costs that such laws impose on non-residents are not large, and may even be smaller than the benefits provided to local residents, those costs are likely to be distributed regressively. Therefore, in terms of their impact on traffic congestion, local growth management ordinances are essentially beggar-thy-neighbor devices.

Part 5
Conclusions

Ten

The Need for Regional Anticongestion Policies

M ANY TACTICS that would be effective in reducing peak-
hour traffic congestion cannot be carried out by individual local governments. These tactics require regional design, implementation, or administration, where "regional" refers to an entire
metropolitan area. In most U.S. metropolitan areas, however, no effective regional governmental agencies exist. Moreover, nearly all local
governments bitterly oppose the creation of such agencies. This chapter explores the tension between the need for regional approaches and
political resistance to them, emphasizing possible ways to overcome
that resistance.

Why Regional Approaches Are Necessary to Reduce Peak-Hour Congestion

As mentioned earlier, anticongestion policies adopted by only one
community are not likely to be very effective—even within its boundaries—unless they are closely coordinated with similar policies
adopted in most other communities nearby. The main exception concerns some policies adopted by very large central cities. Regional
implementation is particularly important for policies focusing on peak-
hour road pricing. No local governments could reduce congestion
throughout a region by adopting peak-hour road pricing solely within
their own boundaries. Regional implementation would also be vital
in establishing a network of high-occupancy vehicle (HOV) lanes,
keeping average settlement densities in areas of new growth above
some minimal level, building new roads or expanding existing ones,
raising gasoline taxes (which requires nationwide action to be most

effective), eliminating free employee parking, and charging a high fee on all vehicles parking during morning peak hours.[1]

Needless to say, some remedies could be effectively carried out by individual local governments acting alone. For example, they could coordinate traffic signals on main streets, institute systems of one-way streets, pressure developers and employers in large job centers to establish traffic management associations, and create roving response teams to clear roadways quickly after traffic accidents. But these tactics would also be much more effective if implemented consistently throughout a metropolitan area.

Furthermore, as noted in chapter 2, peak-hour congestion could best be attacked by using complementary tactics simultaneously. For example, improved traffic signal coordination could be linked to peak-hour road pricing so that traffic diverted from new toll roads would flow efficiently on nearby free-access roads.

Possible Institutional Arrangements

Several kinds of institutional arrangements can be used to carry out regionally coordinated anticongestion policies: (1) voluntary cooperation among legally autonomous local governments, (2) unilateral or coordinating action by state-level transportation or highway departments, (3) comprehensive plan preparation by local planning agencies as part of a state-mandated planning process, (4) establishment of privately run organizations to encourage regional public-private cooperation, (5) establishment of regional public authorities to carry out specific functions, and (6) creation of federal agencies with regional jurisdiction over certain activities.

Voluntary Cooperation among
Autonomous Local Governments

This is the least satisfactory type of arrangement, with the fewest applications to fighting congestion, because it cannot compel local governments to coordinate their behavior closely or to monitor and adjust that behavior. Yet voluntary cooperation could coordinate the upgrading of local streets, the timing of traffic signals, the conversion of local streets to one-way flows, and the creation of roving teams to handle traffic accidents quickly. However, where anticongestion policies require controversial decisions—for example, benefits and costs often have to be allocated across many communities—this arrangement does not work well.

State Transportation or Highway Departments

State transportation or highway departments are already responsible for much transportation facility planning, financing, construction, and operation throughout many metropolitan areas. They have three huge advantages in carrying out regional anticongestion policies: their jurisdictional territory encompasses the entire metropolitan area, unless it includes parts of more than one state; they already possess established capabilities and channels of finance, information, and political influence; and their agencies have access to large continuing flows of money to finance transportation activities and investments.

Therefore such agencies could improve highway maintenance, build new roads or expand existing ones, add HOV lanes to existing roads, coordinate traffic signals, install ramp signals on expressways and arterials, and increase state gasoline taxes. Some state agencies could even install areawide peak-hour road pricing systems—with one proviso. The federal government would have to remove current restrictions on charging peak-hour tolls on interstate highways.[2]

State transportation or highway agencies could also help create cooperative arrangements among local governments to carry out other anticongestion policies, such as charging parking fees during morning rush hours or encouraging the creation of transportation management associations. However, state agencies cannot act without regard for strong political forces. Even where a state agency provides a technically competent vehicle for achieving some policy, that policy will not be carried out unless significant and broad political support for it exists. Hence, state agencies are poor vehicles for instituting new policies that require citizens and officials to change their long-established behavior. Leadership in creating such change rarely comes from public officials in a democracy. They are essentially followers of existing public opinion; in fact, this characteristic is one of democracy's greatest strengths. But it means that adopting new methods—especially controversial ones—requires some other source of change.[3]

*Comprehensive Plan Preparation as Part
of a State-Mandated Planning Process*

Several states require all their local governments to draw up comprehensive land-use plans as parts of their statewide planning systems. These systems are designed to achieve state goals pertaining to the environment, transportation, open space, and housing. The state legislature first establishes broad goals. It then directs all local, county, or regional governments to draw up comprehensive plans pursuing those goals within their own boundaries. This process is normally managed by a state-level agency. It has final coordination and approval power over the plans drawn up by lower-level bodies. By combining state-level goal setting and coordination with detailed local- or regional-level planning, this process uses the best traits of governmental bodies at each level. By late 1991, such processes had been adopted by Oregon, Florida, Georgia, New Jersey, Maine, California, and Vermont. Local compliance was voluntary in Vermont, but compulsory in others, although not always strongly enforced.

Such a comprehensive planning process could be used to carry out certain regional anticongestion policies under some circumstances. One such policy is confining all future urban development to average gross residential densities above some minimum level—say, 2,500 persons per square mile. This would shorten average commuting journeys, compared with those in areas with much lower densities. A state could adopt such a minimum-density policy for all its metropolitan areas. Other anticongestion policies this process might entail are clustering high-density housing near rapid transit and commuter rail stations, stimulating formation of transportation management associations, encouraging more people to work at home, and instituting an areawide peak-hour parking fee.

*Joint Public-Private Coordination, Planning,
and Policy-Promotion Agencies*

Americans have long been noted for forming associations to achieve joint purposes. As Alexis de Tocqueville pointed out: "In no country in the world has the principle of association been more successfully used or applied to a greater multitude of objects than in America."[4] One type especially important in changing public policy has been the public-private organization that transcends individual community boundaries. One example is the United Way organizations that raise and distribute charitable contributions across the nation.

This type of organization has three principal advantages in creating a regional basis for anticongestion policies. First, it can draw together members of both private and public organizations, including business firms, labor unions, nonprofit associations, universities, government agencies, and public legislatures and executives. That is to say, it can provide a forum in which members of these groups come together and discuss joint concerns outside their official organizations. Second, it can establish any geographic jurisdiction its members desire, including entire metropolitan areas. This can be done by a mere declaration of purpose; it requires no official approval by anyone else.

Third, such an agency can take controversial stands without making its individual members commit themselves to those stands. Each member can claim that "the organization" did it or blame all the other members. This permits such an organization to take much more controversial collective positions on issues than many of its members would be willing to endorse individually in public. Hence such an organization is an ideal vehicle for changing public opinion to support some controversial new policy. It can adopt innovative positions ahead of existing public opinion, without exposing its individual members to accusations of ignoring that opinion.

The two main disadvantages of such organizations are that they have little or no money and that they have no governmental powers. Hence they have almost no ability to actually carry out whatever public policies they support, and their roles are confined to influencing public opinion and persuading those who do have money and power to adopt the policies they favor. They can therefore become vehicles for persuading the public and its leaders that some problem is serious enough to demand concerted action; formulating, analyzing, and discussing possible means of remedying that problem; and promoting the specific remedies they believe would be most effective.

These three functions are all vital in securing the adoption of regional approaches to attacking traffic congestion. I believe it is crucial to have some type of public-private regional association outside of government strongly supporting such strategies if they are to be adopted anywhere. If such a regionwide organization already exists to deal with other issues, perhaps it can expand its functions to cope with traffic congestion too. Or else a new organization should be formed for this purpose. The membership should consist of top-level officials in large establishments and other citizens' groups in the metropolitan area concerned, plus governmental leaders who can influence key transportation and land-use policies.

Both private-sector and public-sector leaders should be involved right from the start. They will become unified by sharing in the deliberative process of analyzing congestion problems, examining possible solutions, and arriving at final recommendations. This common experience will secure their emotional commitment to carrying out their final recommendations in the face of the strong resistance sure to arise. Then the organization should launch a concerted campaign of information and political pressure urging the adoption of the regional approaches it has recommended. Examples of such organizations are the San Francisco Bay Area Council, the greater New York Regional Planning Association, and Los Angeles 2000.

Unfortunately, at the time of writing, no such privately sponsored campaigns favoring regional approaches to combat traffic congestion had been successfully carried out anywhere in the United States. A few had been attempted, but none had succeeded.

Specialized Regional Agencies

In some U.S. metropolitan areas, all public transit has been turned over to special regional agencies. They now run the bus lines, commuter rail lines, and fixed-rail mass transit systems. In other areas, regional agencies are responsible for key highway-oriented facilities, such as bridges and tunnels. In the New York City area, the regional Port Authority operates bridges, tunnels, bus terminals and bus lines, port facilities, and the main airports. Where such specialized regional agencies already exist, they can under some circumstances carry out regional anticongestion policies.

For example, regional agencies that run rapid transit and bus systems could improve the service and facilities of those systems to divert traffic from highways. Such agencies could also try to encourage high-density residential and commercial development in the vicinity of their major stations. These tactics are not in themselves likely to reduce congestion signficantly, but they might be useful as parts of a larger and more comprehensive set of tactics.

Where a regional highway agency already exists, its scope for carrying out congestion-reducing tactics is even greater. For example, the agency that operates the Golden Gate and Bay bridges leading into San Francisco could employ peak-hour tolls on both. However, this assumes that the agency has sufficient political courage to raise peak-hour tolls high enough to dissuade many auto commuters from using the bridges. That proviso emphasizes again the importance of creating widespread public support for regional anticongestion policies among citizens and political leaders. It will not do any good to establish the institutional mechanisms to effect those policies unless such support has been generated in advance.

In most U.S. metropolitan areas, no such specialized transportation agency now exists. However, it is certainly easier to create such an agency to attack congestion than to create a general regional government to achieve the same goal. For one thing, the regional nature of transportation problems is so obvious that hardly anyone can dispute it. Moreover, local governments feel much less threatened by regional transportation-oriented agencies than by more general regional governments.

Therefore, persons promoting regional anticongestion strategies should seriously consider setting up some type of regional transportation agency. Ideally, its jurisdiction should include the planning, construction, and operation of the area's principal highways, bridges and tunnels, mass transit systems, and regional parking regulations. Such an agency is easiest to create when the entire metropolitan area lies within a one state. If regional public agencies with the genuine power to affect traffic congestion are ever to be created, this is probably the form most will take.

Federally Rooted Regional Agencies

The federal Clean Air Act provides a potentially powerful regional force that might affect traffic congestion. That law establishes air quality standards for all U.S. metropolitan areas. The federal Environmental Protection Agency (EPA) requires state governments to create plans for cleaning up the air in "nonattainment areas" where air pollution exceeds acceptable levels. Nonattainment areas have boundaries identical with those of metropolitan areas and consolidated metropolitan areas. Therefore, a state can set up a regional organization to coordinate air quality improvement throughout an entire metropolitan area. Moreover, acting through such state-created agencies, the federal government can override or preempt certain local ordinances related to air quality.

Emissions from automotive vehicles are a primary cause of air pollution. Long average commuting trips in general, and traffic congestion in particular, both increase the emissions discharged into the atmosphere. So these air quality improvement agencies have become concerned with traffic flows, especially in California. Consequently, the Southern California Air Quality Management District (AQMD) has drawn up proposed regulations—not yet formally adopted—that would require major changes in driving and commuting behavior over large territories. For example, it has proposed that a significant fraction of all automotive vehicles be powered by fuels other than gasoline by the year 2010. Achieving that goal would require enormous changes both in the automobile and petroleum industries and in household behavior.

Such federally empowered agencies could in theory implement many of the potentially most effective anticongestion tactics at regional levels. For example, they could impose peak-hour road pricing and parking charges throughout a metropolitan area. Therefore, federally rooted antipollution agencies represent one of the potentially strongest instruments for carrying out regional anticongestion tactics. Up to late 1991, however, very few had been established.

Such agencies could adopt and carry out regional anticongestion tactics effectively only if two conditions prevail. First, each agency's leaders must be convinced that specific regional anticongestion tactics are absolutely necessary to reduce their air pollution to acceptable levels. This is not a foregone conclusion. There has been so little experience with regional application of these tactics that no one can be sure just how they would affect air quality. Moreover, there is always a lot of resistance to regional approaches, and so a strong case must be made that these tactics would greatly reduce air pollution before any regional air quality improvement agency will adopt them. Developing such a case is an important task for proponents of anticongestion tactics.

Second, most of the citizenry must voluntarily accept and follow these regulations. Past U.S. experience has repeatedly shown that strong and widespread citizen rejection of laws that require major behavioral changes may severely undermine their effectiveness. This can occur even if the agencies concerned have unchallenged legal authority to pass and enforce such laws. If many citizens ignore or flaunt such laws, it may be impossible for these agencies to enforce them. That happened in connection with the prohibition of alcoholic beverages during the 1920s and early 1930s. It is now happening in the area of drug use. Even massive federally financed efforts to prevent illegal drug distribution and use have not come close to stopping either. A similar defiance of laws governing vehicle speed limits occurs throughout the nation every day.

Thus, widespread citizen opposition to severe limitations on the design, purchase, and use of cars and trucks could very well undermine the effectiveness of federal efforts to impose those limitations. Such opposition would soon be communicated to elected officials, who could restrict the powers of air quality improvement agencies to pass and enforce those laws. Exactly that happened when HOV lanes were first opened on the Santa Monica freeway in Los Angeles, as pointed out earlier. However, it is too soon to predict that this will actually happen if a regional air-quality improvement agency tries to carry out unpopular anticongestion tactics. In spite of potential citizen resistance, the already legally established powers of such agencies to act across an entire metropolitan area provide a potentially effective means of carrying out regional anticongestion tactics.

The above analysis of how to organize regional anticongestion policies does not imply that congestion can best be attacked by creating a single regional agency as the czar of all anticongestion policies. Instead, it might be desirable to have different congestion-reducing policies run by different local and regional agencies that organized themselves in ways best suited to their individual tasks. But if several anticongestion agencies are created at the regional level, they should certainly be linked through both formal and informal coordination.

Likely Opposition to Regional Anticongestion Agencies

In almost every U.S. metropolitan area, attempts to carry out effective regional anticongestion tactics will be met by strong resistance. Any organizations created for this purpose could work well only if they exercised authority and powers now divided among many local and state government agencies, but most officials in those existing agencies strongly oppose any reduction in their present powers.

Local governments are particularly loathe to yield any control over their land uses to outsiders. Indeed, the main function of many U.S. local governments is to control land-use patterns so as to benefit their existing residents. Yet many tactics for reducing peak-hour congestion would require shifting at least some local power over land uses to a regional agency.

Although most local governments will resist the creation of effective regional agencies, state governments would normally not be expected to do so. State governments encompass entire metropolitan areas or large parts thereof; hence they should not exhibit the same narrow parochialism as local governments. In most metropolitan areas, the territory of regional agencies would lie entirely within a single state. And only state governments have the constitutional authority to create such regional agencies. Yet most state governments have been unwilling to create such regional agencies to combat traffic congestion.

One problem is that each such agency would most likely be given powers that are now in part exercised by other state agencies. Officials in those other agencies would be unhappy about giving up any of their present powers. Second, no state legislature is willing to incur the wrath of most local governments unless the legislators have strong incentives to do so. State legislators are themselves elected from local districts. They are often linked personally and politically to existing local governments. Moreover, since state representatives are seldom elected from districts large enough to encompass an entire metropolitan area, their viewpoints are also quite parochial.

At the same time, certain positive gains might motivate state legislators to establish regional anticongestion agencies over the objections of local governments. The main gain would lie in reducing traffic congestion in the long run, but that gain would be spread over residents and firms in all parts of the metropolitan area. For each beneficiary, it would be only a small part of the general benefits received from all state government actions. Hence few beneficiaries would decide how to vote among state legislative candidates on the basis of this issue alone.

In contrast, the potential loss of local sovereignty from the creation of such regional agencies would be seen by many local officials as a major threat to their welfare. So how each state legislator voted on this issue would heavily influence the amount of support he or she received at the next election from local officials. In the minds of most state legislators, the potential loss of support caused by their favoring creation of strong regional agencies would outweigh the gains from reducing traffic congestion.

This does not mean states will never create effective regional anti-congestion agencies, simply that such actions will be rare, and even when they occur, some resistance will persist within both state and local governments. Underlying that resistance is the fundamental belief among many citizens that reducing traffic congestion is far less important than pursuing other social or personal goals. Therefore, if reducing congestion means they must change behavior they have cherished for other reasons, they may prefer to endure congestion—while, of course, still complaining loudly about it.

Conditions of Political Support

What would cause the relevant public officials to adopt such tactics in spite of the above drawbacks? First, traffic congestion must become so widespread and so intolerable that a large fraction of the metropolitan area's citizenry regards it as a crisis. Second, key state and local officials—especially the governor—must believe that carrying out regional anticongestion tactics is essential to remedying this crisis. Third, there must be some credible institutional structure available through which to accomplish those regional tactics.

THE NEED FOR A CRISIS. In a few metropolitan areas, peak-hour congestion is so bad that reducing it is widely perceived as the central issue facing local governments. Hence the governor and state legislators are strongly motivated to appear to be doing something about this problem in order to be reelected.[5] Otherwise, they are unlikely to act effectively, since the political leaders in a democracy fear asking the citizenry to make fundamental changes in established institutions or behavior. People can be induced to do so without enormous resistance only if they believe they must to alleviate a crisis that is either already present or imminent. Elected officials are in turn unwilling to ask the public to make basic changes unless they believe the public thinks itself threatened by such a crisis.

Most such crises involve some sudden disruption of normal life. They must pose serious, obvious, and immediate threats to the welfare

of a large percentage of the population. But peak-hour traffic congestion does not change dramatically overnight; rather, it gets a little
worse each day. Since each commuter's route differs from those traveled by most others, people do not all encounter the same degree
of congestion simultaneously. So there is no widespread common
perception concerning just how bad traffic congestion has become as
of any particular date.

Without any sudden crisis to galvanize public officials into action,
they are reluctant to ask citizens to make the painful changes necessary
to alleviate peak-hour congestion. True, after congestion has become
bad enough long enough, more and more citizens and their political
leaders may decide it has passed some invisible threshold of acceptability. If enough citizens do, some elected officials will propose the
kinds of actions described in this book.

THE NEED FOR A BELIEF THAT REGIONAL REMEDIES ARE
ESSENTIAL. Even then, key officials must be convinced that strong
regional agencies are essential to cutting traffic congestion. Otherwise
they will prefer other remedies not requiring such drastic behavioral
changes. But the belief that regional remedies are essential is not
widespread. A critical function of public-private anticongestion
groups is to nurture and strengthen this belief in the minds of relevant
public and private leaders.

THE NEED FOR CREDIBLE REGIONAL INSTITUTIONS. Even
if the first two conditions exist, one or more credible institutional
structures for implementing regional congestion remedies must also
be available in the metropolitan area concerned. Possible forms of
such structures were discussed above. This condition implies that all
key segments of the metropolitan area must lie within a single state.
If they are in two or more states, it will be extremely difficult to create
any institutional structures able to carry out anticongestion tactics
throughout the region. Rivalries among political leaders and agencies
in different states and the legal difficulties of creating interstate com-
pacts will greatly complicate that task.

This condition also implies that both regional structures and the
widespread belief that they are essential should be created before
traffic congestion produces a crisis. Then when such a crisis appears,
regional policy responses can be launched immediately. That will
permit effective action to start before public concern with the crisis

wanes. This is critical, because the public's attention rarely remains focused on any one issue very long.[6] Therefore, persons promoting effective anticongestion tactics should start building a foundation for regional responses well before congestion reaches maximum intensity.

The Need for Irrational Persistence

In the long run, severe peak-hour traffic congestion can only be effectively combated with the aid of at least some regional anticongestion tactics. But it is extremely difficult to create the political support and institutional structures necessary for such tactics. To do so, proponents of these tactics will have to overcome massive resistance from local governments, existing state agencies, and a majority of citizens who do not want to stop commuting alone in their cars.

To accomplish this task they will have to act in advance of any widely perceived congestion crises. It also demands persisting—perhaps for many years—in spite of continuous failure. After all, not one of the 333 metropolitan areas in the United States has yet adopted a comprehensive, regionally based strategy for attacking traffic congestion, insofar as I know. This does not mean that all efforts to achieve a regional approach should be abandoned as hopeless. But it does mean that persons attempting such efforts must be prepared to endure failure for a long time. Their motto must be, "Never give up!"

Eleven

Summary and Conclusions

DURING THE 1980s, peak-hour traffic congestion became widespread in many U.S. suburban areas. Congestion is especially prevalent in the largest metropolitan areas and in fast-growing ones, particularly in Southern California. At the same time, traffic congestion is not much of a concern in smaller metropolitan areas and other regions containing a majority of the U.S. population.

Reducing congestion is worth doing because traffic jams cost Americans billions of dollars in wasted time and fuel each year and contribute to air pollution. The failure to confront commuters with the true social costs of their driving alone during congested periods has two other ill effects. It understates the cost of living in low-density patterns and leads to an overinvestment in highways. Both outcomes contribute to an excessive spreading out of American metropolitan areas. That raises energy costs, increases infrastructure costs, increases vehicle-miles traveled, and worsens air pollution.

Immediate Causes of Peak-Hour Congestion

The most obvious immediate cause is rapid growth in a metropolitan area's population and employment. Equally important has been a remarkable increase in the ownership and use of automotive vehicles. From 1975 to 1990, the total number of cars and trucks in use throughout the United States rose by 59.2 million, or 49.4 percent, compared with an increase of 32.7 million, or 15.2 percent, in the nation's human population. Hence the number of automotive vehicles per 1,000 persons in 1988 shot up 29.7 percent, from 556 in 1975 to 721.

Another immediate cause of peak-hour congestion has been the unwillingness of U.S. public authorities to build many additional roads during the 1980s, despite the explosion in vehicle ownership and use. In thirty-nine major U.S. urban areas, the number of lane-miles of expressways and major arterial streets combined rose 13.7 percent, but the number of vehicle-miles driven each day increased 31.4 percent.

The final immediate cause has been the perennial failure of society to force vehicle drivers to confront the full costs of their travel during peak hours. Each entrant onto crowded roads adds to traffic congestion, thereby imposing nontrivial losses of time on other drivers there. But each such entrant pays nothing directly for loading that cost onto others. This disparity between individual and collective costs leads to greater congestion than would otherwise occur and decreases national efficiency.

Underlying Causes of Peak-Hour Congestion

Peak-hour traffic congestion is deeply rooted in behavior patterns that reflect certain cherished goals held by most Americans. To reduce congestion it will therefore be necessary to change some of those fundamental behavior patterns, which is a tall order. Most Americans are not even aware of the strong link between traffic congestion—which they hate—and these ingrained behavior patterns—which they love. A central purpose of this book has been to foster a better understanding of this connection.

One long-term cause of congestion is the concentration of commuting trips during certain hours. This is efficient for employers because it permits workers in many organizations to interact during shared business hours. In 1983, however, work-related trips constituted only 50.3 percent of all trips made during the morning rush hours (6 to 9 a.m.) and 31.1 percent of all those made during the evening rush hours (4 to 7 p.m.).

Another underlying cause is workers' desire to enjoy a wide choice of where to live and where to work. The average one-way commuting trip in the United States in 1983 was about 10 miles long and took twenty-two minutes. People select both home and job locations for many reasons besides minimizing commuting travel. Long commutes have been encouraged by the entry of more women into the formal work force. It is not easy for households with two or more workers to choose a home close to all of its members' jobs.

Equally important is the strong desire of most Americans to live in relatively low-density settlements, dominated by detached single-family homes. This desire is a central part of "the American dream" of success. Moreover, the nation's population has steadily shifted both toward the South and the West, and more into suburbs. A rising fraction of all U.S. residents now lives in relatively new urban areas, designed and built during the automobile era. These newer areas have much lower residential densities than older urban areas and can be efficiently served only by individual automotive transportation rather than mass transit. Furthermore, the residents must travel greater distances to conduct their daily lives.

Regional congestion has been greatly affected by the spreading out of workplaces among scattered, low-density establishments, which many suburban zoning ordinances have promoted in recent years. Ironically, such laws are often adopted to limit local traffic congestion generated by high density, but it is much more difficult for workers to use ride sharing or mass transit to reach widely scattered jobs than jobs densely concentrated in a few central nodes.

Most Americans cherish their right to travel in their own private vehicles, usually alone. Ownership of one's own car is a deeply ingrained mark of status. Driving alone also provides a much more convenient, faster, and more comfortable means of commuting than ride sharing, buses, or rapid transit, yet it is also the single biggest cause of peak-hour congestion. In 1983, 68.3 percent of all morning commuters drove alone in automotive vehicles—in comparison with 60 percent in 1977.[1]

The problem is that most Americans do not realize that in pursuing these cherished goals they generate myriad individual vehicle movements during peak hours, thereby producing the congestion they abhor. The cause of peak-hour congestion lies at the door of American suburban development, which has been so successful in achieving its residents' desires. Until more Americans recognize this linkage, it will be impossible to alter their behavior and reduce traffic congestion to any significant degree.

Proposed Remedies for Peak-Hour Congestion

There are two basic kinds of strategies for reducing peak-hour congestion. Supply-side strategies expand the carrying capacity of an area's transportation system. Examples of supply-side tactics are building more roads and improving the service and amenities of public transit. Demand-side strategies reduce the number of trips made on an area's roads during peak hours. Examples of demand-side tactics are imposing higher gasoline taxes, charging high tolls for travel on major roads during peak hours, and clustering high-density housing around transit stops.

Some tactics of both types are primarily *market-based*. They put various monetary prices on different types of behavior and permit each individual to choose whatever behavior he or she is willing to pay for. An example is charging peak-hour tolls on major roadways. Other tactics are primarily *regulatory*. They mandate certain types of behavior and forbid others, without regard to individual preferences. An example is prohibiting employers from offering free parking to their employees. Market-based approaches have the advantage of maximizing individual choice but the disadvantage of favoring high-income households over poorer ones. Many tactics combine both market-based and regulatory elements.

As an economist, I favor market-based approaches whenever possible. However, their political feasibility has been restricted by the egalitarian American desire not to provide any relative advantage to high-income travelers versus low- or moderate-income ones. This desire is politically potent because nearly 90 percent of all U.S. households own and use automotive vehicles. And households considering themselves in the low- and moderate-income category vastly outnumber those considering themselves to have high incomes.

Four Essential Principles of Traffic

To determine how proposed remedies for traffic congestion might actually work, it is necessary to understand four basic principles of traffic.

The *triple convergence principle* states that any large *initial* reduction of peak-hour travel times on a major limited-access roadway will soon be offset by the subsequent convergence on that roadway of drivers who formerly (1) used alternative routes, (2) traveled at other times, or (3) used public transit. Thus, even greatly widening any major commuter expressway cannot long reduce peak-hour congestion there. Additional drivers will shift onto that improved road from other routes, other times, and public transit until movement on it is just as slow as the movement on alternative routes. Since those other routes are less direct than the expressway, such equalization means expressway traffic is usually crawling at the peak hour. Even most wholly new roads will soon fill up during peak hours.

The *principle of the swamping effect of rapid growth* states that relatively small reductions in initial traffic congestion in a rapidly growing metropolitan area will be fully offset within a few years by the arrival of more people, jobs, and vehicles there. Several proposed remedies to traffic congestion can produce only small initial reductions. Such small improvements will be fleeting if the areas where they occur are growing rapidly.

The *imperviousness principle* states that no one suburb can adopt policies that will substantially affect the overall population or job growth of its metropolitan area as a whole. Therefore, if any one suburb limits growth within its own boundaries, the growth prevented there will simply move elsewhere within or near its metropolitan area. But since traffic congestion arises because of movements throughout each metropolitan area, individual communities, except for a few large central cities, cannot greatly affect the total amount of traffic in their metropolitan area by means of their local policies alone. If *all* local communities acted together to limit their growth, they might affect the expansion of the entire metropolitan area, but such concerted action is extremely difficult to arrange in America's fragmented system of local government.

These three principles help explain why it is extremely difficult to reduce peak-hour traffic congestion permanently and doing so probably cannot be done by adopting any one remedy alone, even at a very large scale.[2] Hence the *principle of one-hundred small cuts* states that, just as a woodsman with a small axe can only chop down a large tree with many small blows, a metropolitan area can reduce its peak-hour traffic congestion only by applying many different remedies simultaneously in a coordinated manner.

An Important Behavioral Policy Objective

Although no one remedial tactic is likely to reduce peak-hour congestion substantially, one behavioral change could do so: persuading more commuters now driving alone to share rides with others. This tactic would be effective because the overwhelming majority of daily commuters are persons driving alone. Any sizable doubling-up of these Lone Rangers would reduce the number of daily commuting trips far more than any other single change. Moreover, such doubling-up could occur almost overnight if commuters were motivated strongly enough. This has been shown by sharp shifts in individual travel behavior in Los Angeles during the 1976 Olympic games and in San Francisco right after the 1989 earthquake. This change cannot be achieved on a big enough scale to cut peak-hour congestion appreciably unless many different tactics are used simultaneously.

Data from 1983 indicate that half of all trips in the morning rush hour are work-related, and about two-thirds of all persons commuting to work drive alone. Hence one-third of all trips involve lone drivers. In the evening rush hour, one-third of all trips are work-related, and 60 percent are by solo drivers. Thus about 20 percent of all trips involve lone drivers. Persuading just one-third of these people to share rides would cut the number of peak-hour trips by 11 percent in the morning and 7 percent in the evening.[3] These reductions may seem small, but they could produce dramatic effects on the levels of delay and congestion during peak periods. Moreover, these are much larger trip reductions than would result from any attempts to get more people to use mass transit.

Several different anticongestion tactics could effectively influence more people to share commuting trips in private vehicles. They include peak-hour road pricing, collecting a surcharge for long-term parking during morning peak hours, eliminating free parking provided by employers, and raising gasoline taxes. What makes these tactics effective is that they all greatly increase the costs of driving alone during peak hours.

This is unfortunate because it confronts solo-driving commuters with a dilemma of choosing between two costs, both of which they vehemently oppose. One cost is giving up the benefits of driving alone, which the vast majority of commuters prefer. The second cost is suddenly having to start paying a substantial cash charge for continuing the formerly "free" privilege of driving alone. This is like telling someone who for years has enjoyed drinking clear water without charge from a local spring that she must start either drinking castor oil or paying a hefty price for the water. Neither alternative seems palatable. Nor will most commuters accept either until they become absolutely convinced that present congestion is unbearable and there are no other feasible ways to reduce it.

True, reducing the costs of ride sharing might increase its extent without compelling solo commuters to face the unpleasant choice described above. That could be done through greater availability of HOV lanes and employer provision of benefits to ride-sharing workers. However, these tactics will not cause nearly as many lone drivers to change their ways as forcing them to pay high costs for continuing to commute solo. Hence the best medicines for traffic congestion are also the most difficult to get most commuters to swallow. People resist such remedies partly because most do not realize that their driving alone is the primary cause of peak-hour congestion. Nevertheless, the best litmus test for the potential effectiveness of a proposed remedy for peak-hour congestion is to what extent it would cause greater ride sharing by persons now driving to work alone.

Rating the Desirability of Specific Anticongestion Tactics

This book has analyzed twenty-three different anticongestion tactics to determine their likely effectiveness and social desirability. Because both these qualities have multiple dimensions, it is not easy to summarize the results. But some method of comparing tactics is necessary to help policymakers choose which to pursue most vigorously. Therefore, a rating system has been designed that evaluates each tactic in relation to seven basic traits. These traits plus some comments on how they are used in this system are set forth in the accompanying list of criteria.

These ratings are admittedly subjective rather than scientific; they represent the author's best judgments. That is inescapable: no "purely scientific" method of evaluating such policies can be devised, because doing so inherently requires value judgments. These ratings are not entirely arbitrary, however, since they have been based on the analysis presented earlier. Moreover, by breaking down the rating of each tactic into several categories, this system enables readers to develop their own ratings for specific tactics. They can do so using whatever views about these traits of each tactic they have developed from prior chapters and from their own knowledge and experience.

Criteria for Rating Desirability of Anticongestion Tactics

Effectiveness at Reducing Congestion: How effective would this tactic be at reducing congestion if it were implemented on a large scale?

Extent of effectiveness: What portion of commuting behavior does tactic affect?

Broad: Affects large portion.

Variable: Varies depending on how and under what conditions applied.

Narrow: Affects only a small portion.

Impact of tactic on congestion: Within the portion of commuting behavior this tactic affects, to what extent does it reduce congestion?

Greatly: Reduces congestion to significantly relative to other tactics.

Moderately: Reduces congestion some.

Little: Does not reduce congestion much.

Costs of Implementing Tactic: How expensive is tactic to carry out to achieve maximum effectiveness?

Costs for commuters only: How large are added costs commuters must pay directly?

Great: Will seem significant to commuters.

Moderate: Commuters will pay somewhat higher direct costs.

Minor: Small additional costs for commuters.

None: No additional direct costs for commuters.

Costs to society: How large are the added costs society as a whole (at least within the metropolitan area concerned) must pay? (Can be the same as costs imposed directly on commuters.)

Ease of Implementation: How difficult would it be to establish the institutional and other arrangements to put tactic into effect on a large scale?

Institutional change required: How much change in existing institutional structures would be necessary?

Regional: Agency with regionwide powers would have to be established or existing regional agency used. This would require very difficult institutional change.

Cooperative: Existing institutions could carry out tactic if they cooperated more closely. Moderately difficult change.

None: No major institutional change required.

Ease of administration: How difficult would it be for the institutions carrying out this tactic to make it work and monitor its progress?

Hard: Great difficulty.

Moderate: Moderate difficulty.

Easy: Little difficulty.

Political Acceptability: How strong an *existing* base of political support for adoption of this tactic is there in most U.S. metropolitan areas where congestion is a serious problem?

Good: Sufficient support so that the tactic could be adopted.

Moderate: Some support, but resistance would be strong. Considerable political effort required to get tactic adopted.

Poor: Little support; the tactic would be strongly opposed.

This rating system has been applied to all twenty-three anticongestion tactics. The results are set forth in table 11-1. The twenty-three tactics have been divided into eight supply-side policies and fifteen demand-side policies. Within each group, the table lists these tactics in descending order of the author's view of their likely overall effectiveness—*if* each were applied on a large scale. Some of the tactics near the top of each group have very low ratings concerning costs, ease of implementation, and political acceptability. The next few sections of this chapter discuss various aspects of the tactics and ratings in this table.

General Conclusions Derived from the Ratings Table

One of the more important conclusions about anticongestion tactics derived from table 11-1 is that *very few tactics could greatly reduce traffic congestion by themselves, even if widely applied*. A few others would moderately reduce congestion. But most would have relatively minor effects—if applied alone. That is why a multifaceted approach is so important in attacking congestion.

In general, *supply-side tactics are much more costly to society as a whole than demand-side tactics*. The latter impose most of their costs directly onto commuters to get them to change their behavior. In contrast, supply-side tactics cost commuters little directly, but require substantial social investments. They involve big public spending on facilities like more roads, improved highway maintenance, new HOV lanes, the upgrading of streets, or construction of more transit facilities. Such tactics receive strong political support from industry groups that would benefit from these investments. They include the automobile, road-building, and public transit industries. This is one reason that such tactics have moderately favorable political acceptability. Yet none of the costliest supply-side tactics would greatly reduce congestion; all would have only moderate or minor impacts.

Also, *demand-side tactics generally have broader effects than most supply-side tactics*; that is, they would affect a higher percentage of all commuters to some degree. Yet demand-side tactics are less costly to society as a whole, although they impose more direct costs on commuters.

As a group, *the most effective supply-side tactics would require less traumatic institutional change than the most effective demand-side tactics.* Several of the latter require regional administration or much greater intergovernmental cooperation than now exists. Most supply-side tactics could be carried out without much change in existing institutional arrangements.

Demand-side tactics—including the most effective ones—have poor political acceptability at present whereas supply-side tactics have much better political prospects. The principal reason is that key demand-side tactics work by imposing high costs on solo commuting by private car—and that is how most Americans prefer getting to and from work. These tactics would be extremely unpopular if people knew more about them—although right now, most Americans have never heard of them! Also, supply-side tactics are politically supported by strong interest groups whereas demand-side tactics are not.

Four of the five tactics that involve changing the existing or potential location of jobs or housing would have only a small effect on traffic congestion. Yet they would require difficult institutional changes and take many years to bear even limited fruits.

The above conclusions imply that demand-side tactics would be much more effective at reducing congestion, and less costly to society in general, than supply-side tactics. Nevertheless, the former will be much harder to have adopted than the latter. In fact, political probabilities alone suggest that society is much more likely to attack congestion with supply-side tactics. Such a strategy would produce few results at great cost, compared with demand-side tactics.

The Potentially Most Comprehensive and Effective Remedy

In reality, only two of these twenty-three anticongestion tactics could produce a significant reduction in peak-hour traffic congestion unaided. That is, each could do so by itself—if applied throughout a metropolitan area. These are peak-hour road pricing on major traffic arteries and charging a sizable special fee for *all* parking during morning peak hours.

ROAD PRICING. Peak-hour road pricing has three main advantages over most other tactics. First, it could be fully applied—at least technically, if not politically—within a relatively short time period,

TABLE 11-1. *Ratings of Policies for Reducing Traffic Congestion*

| | Effectiveness | | Costs | | Implementation | | |
Policy[a]	Extent	Impact	Direct to commuters	To all society	Required institution	Ease of administration	Political acceptability
Supply-side							
Rapidly removing accidents	Variable	Great	None	Minor	None	Easy	Good
Improving highway maintenance	Broad	Moderate	None	Moderate	None	Moderate	Moderate
Building added HOV lanes	Variable	Moderate	None	Great	Cooperative	Hard	Moderate
Building new roads without HOV lanes	Variable	Moderate	None	Great	Cooperative	Moderate	Poor
Upgrading city streets	Variable	Moderate	None	Moderate	None	Easy	Moderate
Building new off-road transit systems, expanding existing ones	Narrow	Moderate	Minor	Great	Cooperative	Hard	Poor
Increasing public transit usage by improving service, amenities	Narrow	Minor	None	Moderate	None	Hard	Moderate
Coordinating signals, TV monitoring, ramp signals, electronic signs, converting streets to one way	Narrow	Minor	None	Minor	None	Moderate	Good
Demand-side							
Instituting peak-hour tolls on main roads	Broad	Great	Great	None	Regional	Moderate	Poor
Parking tax on peak-hour arrivals	Broad	Great	Great	None	Regional	Hard	Poor

Policy							
Eliminating income tax deductibility of providing free employee parking	Broad	Great	Great	None	Cooperative	Moderate	Poor
Providing income tax deductibility for commuting allowance for all workers	Variable	Great	None	Minor	None	Easy	Poor
Increasing gasoline taxes	Broad	Moderate	Great	Moderate	None	Easy	Poor
Keeping densities in new growth areas above minimal levels	Broad	Moderate	None	Minor	Regional	Hard	Poor
Encouraging formation of TMAs, promoting ride sharing	Narrow	Moderate	None	Minor	Cooperative	Hard	Moderate
Encouraging people to work at home	Broad	Minor	None	None	None	Moderate	Good
Changing federal work laws that discourage working at home	Broad	Minor	None	Minor	None	Moderate	Moderate
Staggering working hours	Variable	Minor	None	None	Cooperative	Moderate	Moderate
Clustering high-density housing near transit station stops	Narrow	Minor	None	Minor	Cooperative	Hard	Moderate
Concentrating jobs in big clusters in areas of new growth	Narrow	Minor	None	Great	Regional	Hard	Poor
Increasing automobile license fees	Broad	Minor	Moderate	Minor	None	Easy	Poor
Improving the jobs-housing balance	Broad	Minor	None	Moderate	Regional	Hard	Poor
Adopting local growth limits	Narrow	Minor	None	Minor	None	Easy	Good

a. Policies are listed within categories in descending order of effectiveness.

say, no more than five years. None of the tactics involving changes in residential or job density or location have that trait. Second, it would immediately affect *all* peak-hour movements on main arteries, not just work-related trips or local trips. Third, and most important, its initial congestion-reducing effects would not be offset by triple convergence of drivers from other roads, time periods, and modes—because *all users* of those roads would have to pay peak-hour tolls.

Another tactic sharing these traits to a lesser degree would be to place relatively high taxes on gasoline. That could not be done by the metropolitan area; it would require action by states or preferably the federal government. Moreover, its driving-reduction effects would apply to all automotive travel, not just peak-hour trips. (That is an advantage for saving energy and reducing air pollution, but not for reducing peak-hour congestion.)

For all other equally comprehensive tactics except parking fees, such as changing job and housing locations or increasing residential densities, perceptible reductions in congestion would not emerge for many years, if ever. Moreover, their effects would mainly reduce potential *future* increases in congestion, rather than *existing* levels.

Peak-hour road pricing would not be a fault-free remedy, however. It would be difficult to collect tolls on every street; so some traffic avoiding arteries with tolls might cause congestion on nonpriced local streets. Moreover, enforcing the system could heavily burden police departments and courts. Most significant, the political resistance to creating appropriate regional agencies to run such systems is extremely strong.

Even so, the potential advantages of peak-hour road pricing—including the large sums of money therefrom that could be used to improve local transportation systems—are so great that it really should be tried somewhere. The U.S. Department of Transportation ought to finance an areawide experiment with peak-hour road pricing in some moderate-sized but heavily congested metropolitan area. That effort could be similar to the federally funded metropolitan-area housing allowance experiments of the 1970s. Lessons learned from them greatly affected later federal housing policies.

SURCHARGE ON LONG-TERM PARKING DURING THE MORNING PEAK PERIOD. A surcharge on parking would have to cover all employees parking in spaces now provided free by employers. If the charge was large enough, many workers would not be able to afford to continue commuting alone.

This tactic would not affect peak-hour trips that did not end in long-term parking. Examples are interregional truck trips, truck deliveries, local errands, and dropping children at school or with babysitters. These trips constitute a large fraction of all vehicle movements during both morning and evening peak periods, and many drivers who would be affected by peak-hour tolls would escape peak-hour parking charges. To that extent, parking surcharges would be less effective in reducing total peak-hour traffic.

If peak-hour long-term parking surcharges were actually collected everywhere in a metropolitan area, however, auto-driving commuters could not escape by changing to nonpriced routes, as they could escape peak-hour roadway tolls.

Peak-hour parking surcharges are open to the same four criticisms that have been leveled at peak-hour road pricing. First, they would harm the poor more than the nonpoor. Second, using such a surcharge amounts to taxing something that is now provided free to millions of American workers. Third, this surcharge would raise a lot of money that would have to be spent on something. Fourth, equitable administration of such a surcharge would require regionwide management under uniform regulations.

But other criticisms of peak-hour road pricing do not apply to parking surcharges. The latter do not pose great administrative difficulties, since most parking facilities are already taxed by state or local governments (although parking provided free by employers is not). Nor would this surcharge invade individual privacy. Furthermore, a peak-hour parking surcharge could be implemented quickly without any public investment in new equipment or roadway redesign.

The Heart of the Problem

The two main drawbacks of a peak-hour parking surcharge are the same as those of peak-hour road pricing. Americans do not want to pay a monetary price for what they now appear to be getting free—even though in reality they are paying the high price of time lost in congestion. Also, most commuters do not want to give up driving to and from work alone—even though their doing so is the central cause of peak-hour congestion. As Hamlet might have put it if he were a commuter today:

> To drive alone, or to ride share,
> That is the question.
> Whether 'tis nobler in the mind to bear
> The jams and delays of outrageous congestion,
> Or to take passengers against a sea of traffic,
> And by ride sharing, end it.

Up to now, most American commuters still seem to prefer driving alone through a sea of congestion to putting up with the policies necessary to decrease it.

Other Relatively Effective Remedies

Three other anticongestion tactics promise more limited but still significant reductions in *existing* levels of peak-hour congestion. They could have a considerable joint impact if coordinated with other tactics in a metropolitan area.

—*Using roving response teams to speed up the removal of accidents blocking roadways.* Because multiple traffic accidents happen daily in every large metropolitan area, they cause immense total peak-hour delays over the course of a year. Hence this simple tactic can have a substantial impact on average travel time. If could be carried out through existing state highway or transportation departments, or some cooperative arrangement among local governments.

—*Eliminating the income tax deductibility of providing free parking for employees.* This policy could be carried out by Congress with one change in the tax laws. Because of interstate competition for business, states are not likely to change their tax laws in this manner unless Congress provides an umbrella, as it did in the case of inheritance taxes.[4] If employers stopped providing free parking, a prime incentive for driving alone would be removed at one stroke.

—*Providing income tax deductibility for a general commuting allowance.* Congress could implement this tactic by permitting employers to deduct payment of a general commuting allowance to all employees, provided that (1) employees could use it to pay for whatever form of commuting they chose, and (2) employers could not provide free parking to workers but would have to charge a reasonable amount against this allowance. This should be done in tandem with the preceding tactic.

Moderately Effective Tactics Not Costly to Society as a Whole

Some tactics would produce only moderate reductions in traffic congestion, but have the advantage of low costs to society in general. Two of these are also relatively easy to implement and therefore are preferable to other tactics that would also cut congestion only moderately but would impose great costs on society in general.

—*Increasing gasoline taxes*. This tactic would be best carried out by the federal government. It imposes a significant cost on all drivers, thereby pressuring them to reduce all types of trips. This would benefit society as a whole by conserving energy, reducing oil imports, and decreasing air pollution, as well as cutting traffic congestion. The money thus raised could be used to improve transportation facilities. The main disadvantage of this tactic is that it would harm low-income households more than middle- and upper-income households.

—*Encouraging the formation of transportation management associations*. This tactic could be focused on all newly developing businesses and applied in large established job centers. TMAs can be effective at increasing employee ride sharing. The tactic incurs little public expense and does not need to be implemented by public sector regional agencies.

—*Keeping residential densities in areas of new growth above certain minimum levels*. This tactic would only affect *future* congestion levels over a long period, since it can be applied mainly to now-vacant areas as they develop. For that reason, it would not be very expensive but could have significant effects over the long run.

Tactics with a Small Effect but Low Cost

Most anticongestion tactics would have only a small effect on *existing* congestion levels. Nevertheless, those neither costly to society nor terribly hard to implement might be worth carrying out—especially if combined in a comprehensive anticongestion strategy. Nearly every one of them could be accomplished by action at a single level of government, either local, state, or federal.

—*Encouraging more people to work at home.* Employers would have to be persuaded to promote more telecommuting among their workers, which could benefit the employers as well as society in general.

—*Changing federal work laws that discourage working at home.* This is an adjunct to the preceding tactic, but is separable from it.

—*Improving traffic flows through small-scale devices and arrangements.* These include signal coordination, TV monitoring, ramp signals, electronic signs, and one-way streets.

—*Staggering working hours.* This tactic can be accomplished within each large job center by privately coordinated action among key employers.

—*Clustering high-density housing near transit or commuter rail station stops.* This tactic could increase transit usage appreciably if done by enough communities within a metropolitan area.

Moderately Effective Tactics Costly to Society as a Whole

Some tactics would produce only moderate reductions in traffic congestion, but would be quite costly to society in general because they consist of building expensive additional transportation facilities. They are strongly supported by industrial groups that stand to benefit from such investments. Most would not be hard to implement, because they could be carried out through existing institutions, although they would take considerable time to bear fruit. Also, they would be less upsetting to commuters in general than the primary demand-side tactics. For these reasons, elected officials will be tempted to adopt these tactics rather than the potentially more effective and less costly demand-side tactics that their constituents dislike. These probably suboptimal tactics include the following:

—*Improving highway maintenance.* This tactic is less costly to society than the others listed below.

—*Upgrading major city streets.* This tactic expands flow capacity without the great costs of land acquisition required when building wholly new roads or expanding existing ones.

—*Building additional HOV lanes to encourage ride sharing.* It is more expensive but also more effective to build *added* lanes and make them

HOV lanes than to convert *existing* lanes to HOV use. Also, this tactic is superior to expanding existing roads because it persuades drivers to shift from solo commuting to ride sharing.

—*Building new roads, or expanding existing ones, without HOV lanes.* This tactic is among the most widely used, but its effectiveness is greatly weakened by the principle of triple convergence. Also, it does not pressure solo commuters to shift to ride sharing.

—*Increasing public transit usage by improving services and amenities.* This tactic could become quite expensive. It would work best where existing transit systems serve large job concentrations or housing clusters near their stations. However, its potential for reducing suburban traffic congestion is extremely limited even under favorable conditions.

—*Building new off-road transit systems or expanding existing ones.* Such systems are costly but divert relatively few commuters off roadways, especially in fast-growing areas. Yet many metropolitan areas have proposed or are actually building such systems. They are often persuaded by the argument that "every world-class area ought to have one," rather than by cogent analysis of how these systems will actually work.

Ineffective Tactics

Although some may disagree that the tactics in this strategy are ineffective, the analysis in this book suggests they are just not worth doing under most circumstances.

—*Concentrating jobs in big clusters in areas of new growth.* This tactic poses almost insuperable political obstacles. It would require major changes in existing property tax systems, would insert a whole new layer of bureaucratic regulation into real estate development and the choosing of business locations, and would require massive public spending except where fixed-rail systems already exist. It would have little effect on congestion. It could be applied, however, to increase job site densities in large existing suburban activity centers so as to encourage more transit commuting or more ride sharing among the persons working there.

—*Improving the jobs-housing balance.* This tactic probably cannot be achieved through feasible public policies. Trying to apply it might actually reduce the potential supply of affordable housing in a metropolitan area because its major parts—which need to be carried out simultaneously—have different political acceptability ratings. Some would be adopted and some rejected, with a likely negative overall result. Moreover, some of its most sensible goals will be attained through "natural" forces and adaptations over time.

—*Increasing automobile license fees.* Politicians in a democracy where 90 percent of all households own private vehicles will never increase license fees to high enough levels to deter vehicle usage. Therefore, this tactic would impose heavier burdens on low-income households than higher-income ones without causing either to change their commuting behavior.

—*Placing limits on local growth.* This tactic benefits the residents of the communities that adopt such limits, but harms all other communities in the metropolitan area.

Remedies That Require Regional Action

Several of the potentially most effective remedies to peak-hour congestion, such as peak-hour road pricing, must be planned and administered across an entire metropolitan area. If peak-hour tolls were placed only on the roads passing through a single community, even a big one, they would not be able to reduce congestion throughout the entire metropolitan area.

Similar regional—or even broader—planning and administration would be necessary to construct or set aside a network of HOV lanes, eliminate free employee parking, impose a surcharge on peak-hour long-term parking, expand existing road capacity, build new roads, change tax laws to encourage ride sharing, maintain gross residential densities in areas of new growth above some minimum level, and cluster high-density housing near transit or commuter rail stations.

Unfortunately, few U.S. metropolitan areas have effective governmental institutions at the regional level. Even so, six different organizational arrangements could be used to carry out such anticongestion tactics, depending on the situation.

—*Voluntary cooperation among autonomous local governments.* This would work only for tactics that did not involve controversial decisions or the allocation of costs and benefits among many communities.

—*State transportation or highway departments.* In metropolitan areas lying within a single state, these agencies could carry out the regional administration of several anticongestion tactics: building roads, adding new HOV lanes to existing roads, improving highway maintenance, and helping localities coordinate small-scale traffic flow devices. In some cases, these agencies could administer the construction of new off-road transit systems or the expansion of existing ones. However, state agencies are not willing to carry out any such tactics if strong local opposition to them exists in much of the metropolitan area.

—*State and local planning agencies acting under state comprehensive planning systems.* A few states have adopted comprehensive planning systems that require each local government to draw up a land-use plan serving goals established at the state level. A state agency has final coordinating and approval powers over all locally prepared plans. This system could be used to carry out such tactics as keeping residential densities in areas of new growth above some minimum level, clustering high-density housing near transit stops, concentrating jobs in nodes, and improving the jobs-housing balance. Unfortunately, most of these land-use tactics can do little to reduce existing congestion.

—*Private coordination, planning, and policy-promotion organizations.* In many metropolitan areas, private sector leaders have formed umbrella organizations to study the future problems likely to be caused by regional growth. Members include leaders from private firms, non-profit entities, civic groups, unions, universities, and public agencies. These organizations have little money and no governmental powers. But they can act as a forum for joint deliberations among their members about what regional problems will emerge and what to do about them. Such organizations can adopt much more controversial stands on issues than their members could individually. They can therefore perform important functions in both designing regional policies and helping garner public support for such policies. Examples are the Regional Planning Association in New York, the Bay Area Forum in the San Francisco area, and Los Angeles 2000. Strong leadership from such organizations is probably essential to getting innovative and controversial policies like peak-hour road pricing adopted in any area.

—*Specialized regional government agencies.* These groups are usually transportation-oriented organizations, such as New York City's Port Authority. They have regional powers over varied sets of transportation or infrastructure functions. Where they now exist, they could carry out several types of regional anticongestion policies. And in some metropolitan areas, new agencies of this type could be formed to concentrate on reducing traffic congestion.

—*Federally rooted regional agencies.* In Southern California, the need to carry out the federal Clean Air Act has generated regional Air Quality Management Districts connected to the Environmental Protection Agency through the state government. Because of the sweeping powers granted to EPA under that law and the close connection between vehicle usage and air pollution, such agencies could carry out certain anticongestion tactics over entire metropolitan areas. This provides a potentially powerful vehicle for achieving regional anticongestion tactics *without* the need to gain the approval of a host of local governments.

These organizational forms present many channels through which regional anticongestion tactics might be carried out. However, there must be widespread political support for these tactics if they are to be effective. Even federally mandated policies to improve air quality will not work if they encounter massive public resistance.

Unfortunately, resistance to effective regional administration of anticongestion tactics—or any other policies—is extremely strong in most metropolitan areas. A primary goal of almost all U.S. local governments is to control land-use patterns to serve the interests of their existing residents. Yet many tactics for reducing peak-hour traffic congestion would require shifting at least some power over local land uses to a regional agency. Even anticongestion policies not directly controlling land uses could have an immense impact on just what land uses would develop in each part of a region. Hence local governments are reluctant to yield any power of approval over transportation facilities within their boundaries to a regional agency with broad goals. Since state legislators and administrators also have strong roots in local governments, they hesitate to create strong regional agencies, even though they have the legal power to do so. Therefore, up to now, few regional anticongestion tactics have been effectively carried out anywhere in the United States.

Conditions of Political Support

Public officials might adopt such tactics, in spite of the likely resistance, in certain circumstances.

First, traffic congestion must become so widespread and so intolerable that a large fraction of the metropolitan area's citizenry regards it as a crisis. Elected officials in our democracy almost never have the courage to ask citizens to change their behavior unless there is an obvious and compelling need to do so. However, traffic congestion does not normally generate crises. The intensity of congestion changes too slowly and varies too greatly among individuals to create a widespread public belief that congestion has suddenly become a dire disaster threatening society. Even though many citizens complain bitterly about congestion, it has not yet become intolerable enough to create this condition—at least not in most parts of the nation.

Second, important state and local officials—especially the governor—must believe that carrying out regional anticongestion tactics is absolutely essential to remedying this crisis. Otherwise, they will first pursue other tactics less upsetting to their constituents, but also much less likely to reduce congestion. Few really understand what causes congestion and what remedies might alleviate it.

Third, there must be some credible institutional structure available through which to implement those regional tactics. In practice, two conditions must be fulfilled here. First, the entire metropolitan area must lie within a single state; then a single state legislature can either form new regional organizations to carry out the required anticongestion tactics or give the necessary powers to one or more existing organizations. Metropolitan areas that encompass parts of several states pose extreme legal and administrative difficulties for any such cohesive regional approach. Second, the groundwork for effective implementation of this type should be established *before* a congestion crisis occurs. Leaders in the community, and the public in general, should have become persuaded that curing traffic congestion does indeed require regional remedies. Moreover, it would also be desirable to have the proper institutions legally established in advance. Then, when congestion approaches the crisis level, regional anticongestion actions can be launched almost immediately. Otherwise it may take so long to get them started that the public will have shifted its concern to other matters, and political support for regional attention will no longer exist. Given the tendency of public and media attention to shift rapidly from one subject to another, this is a serious problem.

Conclusion

In many U.S. metropolitan areas, peak-hour traffic congestion is a socially suboptimal condition that wastes billions of dollars worth of time and fuel each year and surely adds to air pollution. Its causes are rooted in several long-established goals and cherished behavior patterns of Americans. Yet most citizens do not realize these prized elements of their lives are generating the traffic congestion they hate. The behavior they value that is most to blame for peak-hour congestion is driving to work alone. Any effective remedies must change that behavior among thousands of commuters. That means getting more of them share rides, use transit, or travel at nonpeak hours. All the workable means of accomplishing these objectives would raise the costs of solo commuting during peak hours. These means include peak-hour road pricing, surcharges on peak-hour long-term parking, and abolishing free employee parking.

Naturally, the patient does not enjoy the prospect of taking such bitter medicine. In fact, the patient regards driving to work alone without paying any fee as an established right and views any interference with it as an uncalled-for blow to his or her welfare. Thus, whether peak-hour congestion can be significantly reduced boils down to three questions. Is traffic congestion widely perceived as being bad enough for most commuters to accept this medicine? Do they understand that only this rather painful cure will work—less painful ones will not help much? Will their anticongestion feelings be strong enough to cause elected politicians to overcome the entrenched resistance of local governments to regional and other anticongestion tactics?

Up to now, the answer to all these questions throughout the United States has clearly been No! However, the strength of anticongestion sentiments is rising rapidly in many areas, and the opportunities for change are greater than ever before. Nevertheless, a considerable degree of peak-hour congestion is almost sure to persist throughout the foreseeable future in all metropolitan areas already experiencing it. That is likely even if the most effective anticongestion tactics are launched there. Those tactics may reduce congestion significantly, but they will probably fail to eradicate it anywhere soon, if ever.

Therefore, my advice to American drivers stuck in peak-hour traffic is not merely to get politically involved, but also to learn to enjoy congestion. Get a comfortable, air-conditioned car with a stereo radio, a tape player, a telephone, perhaps a fax machine, and commute with someone who is really attractive. Then regard the moments spent stuck in traffic simply so an addition to leisure time.

Appendixes

Appendix A

Graphic Analysis of Peak-Hour Road Pricing

How congestion tolls increase economic efficiency is depicted in figure A-1.[1] The solid line *PB* is the demand curve for the use of a commuter expressway. It shows the *average* monetary amount (measured on the vertical axis) that motorists would pay to travel on a highway at any given number of vehicles per lane per hour (measured on the horizontal axis). *PB* is a monetary measure of the average private benefit motorists receive from using the highway. As traffic on the highway rises to more vehicles per lane, this average benefit declines because of increased congestion.

The solid line *MC* shows the private costs incurred by one additional driver at each level of traffic per lane per hour. These costs include auto operating costs plus a monetary value on the time required. As long as the number of vehicles per lane remains below *OQ*, this cost remains constant. That means adding more vehicles in the range *OQ* does not slow the flow of traffic. But when the number of vehicles per lane per hour passes *Q*, congestion begins to reduce average speed. That adds to the time required by the trip, so the cost *borne by each added driver* rises along the solid curve *MCEJ*. The entry of every additional driver also adds to the delays of all other drivers; so the *average total additional cost* for all drivers from entry of one additional driver is greater than the cost borne by the added driver (when no peak-hour tolls are charged). This marginal cost of adding another commuter is shown by the curve *MCAF*. These two costs were identical along the curve *MC*, but diverge beyond traffic volume *OQ*.

The inefficiency of no-fee driving on congested roads arises because each driver does not have to pay the total costs his or her arrival adds to the overall situation. Guided only by the costs they must bear directly, drivers keep entering the road as long as that cost—shown

FIGURE A-1. *Economics of Peak-Hour Road Pricing, Welfare and Traffic Effects of Tolls*

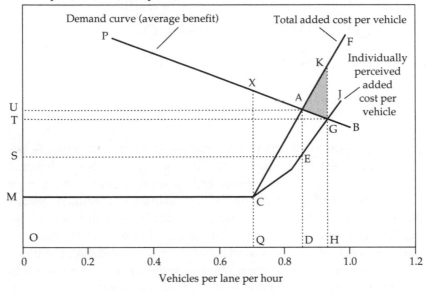

by the curve *MCEJ*—is below the demand curve, *PB*. Hence traffic per lane keeps rising up to level *OH*. But it would be socially more efficient for traffic to be limited to the level *OD*. There the total added cost per vehicle—measured by *MCAF*—crosses the demand curve *PB* at *A*. At that level of traffic, the average total costs imposed by each additional driver—line *MCAF*—are equal to the average total benefit received by all drivers—line *PB*. Higher traffic volumes cause more costs per driver than the benefits they provide per driver; hence they are not socially efficient.

This inefficiency can be measured on the graph. Every added vehicle from traffic level *OD* to traffic level *OH* causes a total added vehicle cost lying along the line segment *AK* (part of curve *MCAF*). Those added costs all exceed the benefits provided by such travel, which are measured by the line segment *AG* (part of curve *PB*). For example, at traffic level *OH*, the total added cost per vehicle is *HK*. That cost exceeds the added benefit per vehicle, *HG*, by the amount indicated by *GK*. Thus, the shaded area lying within the triangle connecting points *A*, *K*, and *G* is a geometric measure of the net collective welfare loss because traffic rises all the way to level OH, instead of stabilizing at level OD.

In order to stop traffic volume from rising beyond level OD, it is necessary to raise the cost borne by an additional driver at that traffic level, DE, to the level DA. This cost increase can be achieved by charging a peak-hour toll for entering or using the roadway. That toll should equal the difference between DA and DE, or the amount AE. On the left-hand axis, this equals the price SU. If toll SU (or AE) is added onto the individually borne costs DE, then the total cost faced by each additional driver equals DA (or OU). Then individual drivers will stop entering the expressway at traffic volume OD, since the costs they would bear by doing so at higher volumes—to the right of point A on $MCAF$—are higher than the benefits they would receive—points on curve PB to the right of A. Thus, the economically optimal toll is EA or SU, and the economically optimal traffic volume is OD.

This traffic volume is *not* the same as the volume with the lowest level of congestion. That would be any traffic volume up to OQ. After that volume level, rising congestion slows down traffic—but not enough to offset the advantages to drivers of using this more direct route.[2]

Appendix B

Translating Gross Residential Densities into Net Residential Densities

CHAPTER 6 discusses mainly *gross residential densities*, that is, thousands of total residents per overall square mile of land. This definition includes *all* land within the community, regardless of its uses, as part of the area concerned. But most Americans who deal with land-use policies conceive of densities in terms of *net residential densities*, that is, numbers of dwelling units per net residential acre. This definition includes *only residential land* in its base; it excludes even local streets and parks in residential neighborhoods and all land used for nonresidential purposes.

Unfortunately, there is no simple or well-established way to relate these two different density measures, because circumstances vary widely from one location to another. For convenience, this appendix presents a method of converting either of these measures into the other.

Two variables are especially crucial in these computations. One is the number of residents per dwelling unit, roughly equivalent to persons per household. The other is the proportion of total land area within a community devoted to residential use, as opposed to streets, highways, parks, open space, commercial uses, and public buildings.

The number of persons per dwelling unit is normally smallest in high-density neighborhoods within large cities, such as New York City. It rises in suburban communities where families with children are more concentrated. Similarly, the percentage of total land area devoted to housing is lowest in big-city neighborhoods that feature mixed-use development. It is highest in the peripheral fringe areas where large-lot zoning is dominant. This variation can be shown from data describing average residential densities in the New York region, taken from *Public Transportation and Land Use Policy*, by Boris S. Push-karev and Jeffrey M. Zupan.[1] They list thirty-five communities in descending order of average dwellings per acre of residential land. The highest is 210.7 in Manhattan, the lowest 1.28 in Sussex County.

Pushkarev and Zupan translate these net residential densities into gross persons per square mile, derived from actual data. For example, the Manhattan gross density is 69,333 persons per square mile of total land area. If every household contains 2.0 persons, then this link of 210.7 dwellings per net residential area and 69,333 persons per gross square mile implies that 25.8 percent of the land is devoted to residential uses.[2] A similar calculation concerning Sussex County's 1.28 dwellings per net residential acre and 147 persons per gross square mile—but using 3.5 persons per dwelling—implies a residential land percentage of 50.15 percent. Other areas between these net density extremes imply even higher residential land coverage ratios, as high as 63 percent. So their calculations imply that the percentage of all land devoted to residential uses varies from a low of 25 percent in highly dense urban areas to a high of over 60 percent in some low-density outlying areas.[3]

For purposes of this analysis, an average household size of 2.5 persons is used, since that is close to the 1990 U.S. average household size of about 2.6. Also, a variable residential land coverage factor is employed: 25 percent for relatively high gross densities (usually 15,000 persons per square mile or higher); 37.5 percent for moderate gross densities (about 5,000 to 14,999 persons per square mile); and 50 percent for relatively low gross densities (usually under 5,000 per square mile).

Table B-1 shows conversions from gross to net densities in the first four columns. The next four columns convert back from net to gross densities, using values derived from the first two columns. Each conversion table employs three different fractions of total land area devoted to residential use, for high-, moderate-, and low-density ranges. Multiple values are computed for densities that might be considered in more than one of these three categories, thus permitting readers to use their own discretion in those overlapping ranges. This table may be referred to in order to clarify parts of the book that refer mostly to gross residential densities. However, the data in this table represent an approximation, not a rigid rule.

TABLE B-1. *Residential Density Conversion*[a]

| | Converting from gross residential density to net residential density | | | | Converting from net residential density to gross residential density | | |
| | Dwellings per net residential acre | | | | Residents per gross square mile | | |
Residents per gross square mile	High density (25 percent of land residential)	Moderate density (37.5 percent of land residential)	Low density (50 percent of land residential)	Dwellings per net residential acre	High density (25 percent of land residential)	Moderate density (37.5 percent of land residential)	Low density (50 percent of land residential)
80,000	200.00	...	...	200	80,000	...	...
60,000	150.00	...	...	150	60,000	...	...
50,000	125.00	...	...	100	40,000	...	...
40,000	100.00	...	...	75	30,000	...	...
25,000	62.50	...	...	50	20,000	...	...
20,000	50.00	33.33	...	40	16,000	...	...
15,000	37.50	25.00	...	35	14,000	...	...
12,500	31.25	20.83	...	30	12,000	...	...
10,000	25.00	16.67	...	25	10,000	...	...
7,500	...	12.50	...	20	8,000	12,000	...
6,000	...	10.00	7.50	15	6,000	9,000	...
5,000	...	8.33	6.25	10	4,000	6,000	...
4,000	...	6.67	5.00	7.5	...	4,500	...
3,000	...	5.00	3.75	7	...	4,200	...
2,500	...	...	3.13	6	...	3,600	4,800
2,000	...	...	2.50	5	...	3,000	4,000
1,500	...	...	1.88	4	...	2,400	3,200
1,000	...	...	1.25	3	...	...	2,400
500	...	...	0.63	2	...	...	1,600
				1			800
				0.5			400
				0.25			200

Source: Author's calculations.

a. Assumes an average of 2.5 persons per dwelling unit. Conversions are computed from gross to net, then extrapolated back from net to gross. More than one value has been calculated in adjacent columns for net densities near the transition points between the three levels of neighborhood density.

Appendix C

A Spatial Model for Simulating Changes in Residential Density and Home and Workplace Locations

THE POTENTIAL impacts on commuting travel of changing the location of jobs or housing can be grasped intuitively without detailed quantitative analysis, as shown in the text of chapters 6 and 7. But logical proof for the resulting conclusions, plus assessing their sensitivity to specific changes in variables, requires detailed quantitative analysis. This can be accomplished by using a spatial model of a typical metropolitan area.

The Basic Model

The model employed in this book consists of a variable-sized square settled area measuring a maximum of 40 miles on each side, as shown in figure C-1. A square is used instead of a circle to simplify calculations of commuting distances. Its maximum area (1,600 square miles) is divided into an inner central city square measuring 12 miles by 12 miles, older suburbs extending outward from the city's boundary to a square 24 miles on each side, and newer suburbs—exurbs—extending outward from the boundary of the older suburbs to a square with variable boundaries but a maximum of 40 miles on each side.

There are thirteen job centers in the basic version of this metropolitan area; all jobs are located in these centers.[1] They include the central business district in the area's center, four other in-city job clusters at the centers of each city quadrant, four suburban job clusters each located 3 miles horizontally and vertically from the outer corners of the older suburban area, and four exurban job clusters located 6 miles horizontally and vertically from the outer corners of the 40-mile-square

FIGURE C-1. *Model Work Trip Area Maps*

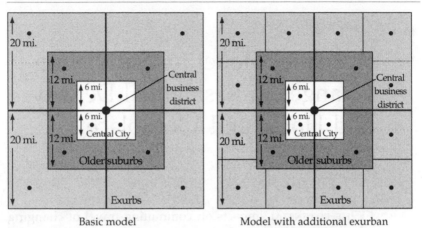

Basic model

Model with additional exurban
job centers

area. However, in the spatially largest cases—those in which the exurbs extend throughout a square 40 miles on a side—there would undoubtedly be more than just four exurban job sites. So a second version has been created with two added job sites in each exurban quadrant. They lie 2 miles horizontally or vertically beyond the boundaries of the suburban zone, and in the middle of their subzones in the other dimension. (To simplify calculations, only exurban-resident workers are employed in these eight added sites; no suburban- or city-resident workers commute there.) This addition creates a total of twenty-one job centers.

Various spatial distributions of population and jobs can be simulated by changing the outer boundaries of the model and changing the proportions within the central city, older suburbs, and exurbs of (1) total jobs, (2) total population, and (3) the percentage of all workers employed in each job center. Workers' homes are spread across the entire area—although at different average densities in the city, suburbs, and exurbs. The average commuting distance from the center of each residential square mile to each job center can calculated algebraically.[2]

Three different types of simulation are used. The first compares fully developed metropolitan areas that have different urban densities. A given total population is divided into three subgroups: central-city residents, suburban residents, and exurban residents. The first two subgroups remain constant in area, total population, and therefore in density throughout the analysis. The exurban subgroup remains constant in total population, but has varying area and therefore varying density. This type of simulation examines the impact of varying exurban densities on average commuting distances. Of course, spatially large metropolitan areas would have more job centers in their outer areas than smaller metropolitan areas. This outcome is simulated by adding more exurban job centers to models that extend quite far out, and by varying the percentage of workers assigned to different job centers.

A second type of simulation starts with a total population and all jobs divided between the central city and suburban regions, but no residents or job centers in the exurbs. It then assumes a certain annual rate of total population growth over an entire decade and places all that growth in the exurbs. By confining that exurban growth to areas of different sizes—and therefore densities—this simulation can examine the impact of varying densities of *future growth* on average commuting distances in already established metropolitan areas. Future population growth rates can also be varied within this model.

A third type of simulation examines changes in the distribution of population or jobs within a metropolitan area of a given size and suburban-exurban configuration. It can be used to analyze certain shifts in the jobs-housing balance.

Initial Calibration of the Basic Model

The largest version of the model consists of a square with 40 miles on a side, divided into zones, as described above. It makes use of all twenty-one job sites. This version has initially been populated and calibrated to resemble large U.S. metropolitan areas in population, number of jobs, population densities, and commuting travel times by various subgroups. Data from various travel surveys and censuses have been used to determine targets that would resemble a typical large U.S. metropolitan area. Census data do not differentiate between exurbs and suburbs; both are combined in a category called "not in a central city." Hence the simulation results for exurbs and suburbs are shown both combined and separately. The calibration for the base-case version of the 40-mile-square model containing population in both suburbs and exurbs is shown in table C-1.[3] This table also presents average commuting distances for different groups of workers as calculated by the model, discussed further below.

TABLE C-1. *Calibration of the Base Model*

Attributes	Model	U.S. SMSAs
Total population (millions)	3.240	Varies
Percentage of population in central city	33.3	Varies
Percentage of population in suburbs and exurbs	66.7	Varies
Jobs as percentage of population (6 percent unemployment)	47.78	47.78
Total number of jobs (millions)	1.548	Varies
Percentage of jobs[a]		
Central business district	8.0	8.4
Central city outside central business district	34.0	39.0
Total central city	42.0	47.4
Suburbs and exurbs	58.0	52.5
Average one-way commuting distance (miles) for workers living in suburbs and exurbs, working in	12.38	12.10[b]
Central business district	18.87	19.70[b]
Central city outside central business district	14.87	15.70[b]
Total central city	15.65	16.50
Suburbs and exurbs	11.30	10.75
Average one-way commuting distance (miles) for workers living in central city, working in	8.71	9.00[b]
Central business district	5.29	10.75
Central city outside central business district	6.13	7.50
Total central city	5.97	8.10[b]
Suburbs and exurbs	17.97	12.00
Average one-way commuting distance (miles) for all metropolitan area workers	11.04	11.00[b]
Population densities per square mile		
Central city	7,875	Varies
Suburbs and exurbs	1,446	Varies
Overall meropolitan area	2,025	Varies

Source: Author's calculations.

a. Data for large urban areas, 1980.

b. Extrapolation. See appendix C, text note 3.

This base-case version of the model has 33.3 percent of the total population living in the central city, 50 percent in the older suburbs, and 16.7 percent in the more distant exurbs. Because of the different areas of these zones, they have widely varying population densities. The central city has an average density of 7,500 persons per square mile, similar to the densities of Los Angeles, Hartford, Detroit, and Buffalo. The suburbs have an average density of 3,750 persons per square mile—one-half that of the central city. This density is similar to that of Lansing, Omaha, Brownsville, Richmond, and Portland, Oregon. The exurbs in the 40-mile-square case have a very low average density of 527 persons per square mile—much lower than that of any large U.S. city. However, when the overall size of the settled area—and therefore of the exurbs —is reduced in subsequent model cases, this exurban density rises significantly.

It is assumed that the population generates workers at the same rate per 1,000 residents in each zone; hence the percentage distribution of workers among these three zones *by residence* is the same as the distribution of population. But jobs are not distributed in the same way as population. So a key step in developing the model is assigning percentages of total jobs to each zone. One fundamental assumption is that the central city contains a higher percentage of total jobs than it does of total residents, because some net inward commuting still occurs, especially to the central business district. Another fundamental assumption is that the suburbs contain a slightly higher percentage of total jobs than of residents, since they attract workers inward from the exurbs. So the exurbs contain a much smaller percentage of total jobs than total residents.

These assumptions have led to the arbitrary—but presumably reasonable—assignment in the 40-mile-square base case of 5 percent of all jobs to exurban job centers, 55 percent to suburban job centers, and 40 percent to central city job centers—including 8 percent to the central business district. This assignment is then translated into specific numbers of jobs from each residential zone into each employment zone by means of a matrix shown in table C-2. This matrix is a vehicle for making the residential and job assignments mutually consistent. It serves as a basis for assigning specific percentages of all metropolitan area jobs to each job center in each of the model's three basic modules: one showing where all exurban-resident workers are employed, and

TABLE C-2. *Matrix of Job Locations and Worker Residence*

| Job location | Worker residence | | | |
	Central city	Older suburbs	Exurbs	Total SMSA
Exurbs				
Number	7,740	23,220	46,440	77,400
Percent	0.5	1.5	3.0	5.0
Older suburbs				
Number	197,060	526,320	128,020	851,400
Percent	21.73	34.0	8.27	55.0
Central business district				
Number	63,468	54,180	6,192	123,840
Percent	4.1	3.5	0.4	8.0
Outside central business district				
Number	247,680	170,280	77,400	495,360
Percent	16.0	11.0	5.0	32.0
Total city				
Number	311,148	224,460	83,592	619,200
Percent	20.1	14.5	5.4	40.0
Total SMSA				
Number	515,948	774,000	258,052	1,548,000
Percent	33.33	50.0	16.67	100.0

Source: Author's calculations. See text.

two others showing where all suburban-resident workers and city-resident workers are employed. These modules are then aggregated into a metropolitanwide summary module and another summary module combining suburban and exurban job assignments.

Base-Case Computation of Commuting Distances

The simulation starts by assigning a certain percentage of all city-resident, suburban-resident, and exurban-resident workers to each job center. This is done from the perspective of a single quadrant in the entire model (the upper left-hand or northwest quadrant), assuming that residents of all four quadrants would have identical behavior patterns. In the 40-mile-square case, each exurban quadrant has three job centers; in other cases with smaller exurban areas, each exurban quadrant has only one job center. Given these assignments, a single average commuting distance can be computed for all exurban-resident workers, another for suburban-resident workers, and another for all city-resident workers. These three averages can be altered by shifting the percentage distributions of workers among job centers *within* each category of centers. For example, shifting more of the total 8.27 percent of exurban-resident workers who are employed at suburban job sites from distant sites to closer ones reduces the average commuting distance for exurban workers. If such within-category shifts do not produce the desired results, the basic allocation of workers among zones can also be changed. The average commuting distance for all workers is then obtained by aggregating the separate calculations for city and suburban residents.

In the 40-mile-square base case, the average commuting distance for all metropolitan area workers is 11.04 miles, as shown in table C-1. This is identical to the actual 1983 average for metropolitan areas containing more than 3 million residents. The average commuting distance for workers living in the central city is also the same in both the model and the data from *Personal Travel in the U.S.* The average from the model for exurbs and suburbs combined is slightly lower than that extrapolated from *Personal Travel in the U.S.* for all residents of large metropolitan areas not in central cities. The shortest average commuting distances from the model are for workers both living and working in the exurbs, workers both living and working in the suburbs, and workers both working and living in the central city (5.47 miles, not shown on the table). These simulation results are consistent with travel-time data that show the shortest commuting travel times in 1980 were for workers both living and working in the suburbs (which are equivalent to the exurbs and suburbs combined in the model).[4]

Exploring the Impacts of Higher Exurban Densities

What impacts on average commuting distances would result from the settlement of the exurbs at higher average densities? A higher-density exurban population can be simulated by confining the same overall population to a total area 30 miles square. In that case, the average density in the exurban area rises to 1,667 persons per square mile —3.16 times the analogous density in the 40-mile-square case. The overall density for the entire metropolitan area rises to 3,600 from

2,025 in the 40-mile-square case. Moreover, because the exurban area is much smaller in this case, only one job center is used in each exurban quadrant instead of four; so the total number of job centers drops from twenty-one to thirteen.

Under these conditions, the average commuting distance for all metropolitan area workers declines—but only to 10.99 miles. Hence, a 216 percent rise in exurban population density, causing a 78 percent rise in average metropolitan density, produces only a 3.6 percent decline in average overall commuting distance. One reason is that the elimination of eight exurban job centers partly offsets the smaller total area of the exurbs. Yet this change reflects the reality that more job dispersal would occur if the exurbs occupied 1,024 square miles (the first case) than 324 square miles (the second case). Hence the average commuting distance for all exurban- and suburban-resident workers falls only 2.6 percent from 12.3 miles to 11.98 miles.

This analysis emphasizes an important but not obvious factor: the impact of greater dispersion of job sites in much larger exurban areas. Even though workers' homes are spread over much larger territories in low-density settlements, this need not generate proportionally longer commuting trips if jobs also become spread out more broadly. Given recent decentralizing trends in office construction, computers, and telecommunications, such a greater dispersal of jobs is quite likely.

To shorten average commuting distances significantly, much higher exurban or suburban densities must be employed. One possibility would be concentrating the entire 66.7 percent noncity population within the older suburbs, thereby eliminating all exurban residences and job centers. The distribution of jobs would also have to be changed, say, to 60 percent in the suburbs and 40 percent in the central city. Population density in the suburbs would rise to 5,000 persons per square mile, one-third higher than in the 40-mile-square base case. That is about the same density as St. Paul, Modesto, Cleveland, and Pasadena. The overall noncity population density would rise from 1,484 in the base case to 5,000 in the 24-mile-square case, an increase of 237 percent. Surprisingly, in these models, this greater concentration of population would reduce average commuting distances for the entire metropolitan area only from 11.2 to 11.04 miles, or by 1.4 percent.[5] The elimination of longer commutes by city and suburban residents to exurban job centers just offsets the movement of population from distant exurbs to closer-in suburbs.

Even higher densities are needed to cut average commuting distances notably. One way to get higher density is to reduce the size of the total settled area to a square 18 miles on a side. That cuts the area occupied by the older suburbs, as well as eliminating exurbs. This decreases the suburbs from 432 square miles to 180 square miles, thereby raising average density from 5,000 to 12,000 persons per square mile. That is the same as the densities of the central cities of Boston and Philadelphia. The percentage distribution of jobs among suburban and city job sites remains the same. This increase in density alone cuts the average commuting distance for the entire metropolitan area to 8.14 miles.

Moreover, in such a suburban settlement of reduced size, suburban job centers are likely to be more centrally located than if left at their coordinates from the 40-mile-square model. Hence each was moved two miles diagonally closer to the downtown before travel distances were computed. The combination of higher density and closer suburban sites reduces the overall average commuting distance for the metropolitan area to 6.64 miles. That is a considerable reduction in commuting travel. It is 41 percent less than the original 40-mile-square base case, and 40 percent less than the 24-mile-square case with a suburban density of 5,000 persons per square mile.[6]

This analysis implies that major reductions in commuting travel can be achieved by raising overall suburban residential densities above typical American levels—but only if the density increases are substantial indeed. Yet most older suburban parts of U.S. metropolitan areas are already built up at not-very-high densities. It would be extremely difficult to alter their densities without encountering massive political and economic resistance from existing residents. This shifts the focus of the analysis to coping with future population growth.

Possible Densities for Future Exurban Development

Another way to analyze the relationship between residential densities and commuting travel is to examine alternative patterns of future exurban growth around essentially unchanging central city and suburban zones. The first step is to assume a certain rate of population and job growth over the next decade, and then convert that rate into absolute gains. The second step is examining the travel distance impacts of having that growth occur at different densities. The model described above is used for these simulations. However, the initial situation is different from that in the previous discussion. In this type of analysis, the entire initial population of 3.24 million is assumed to reside wholly within the central city and suburbs, 35 percent in the city and 65 percent in the suburbs.

This is identical with the previous situation in which the entire settlement pattern was confined to a square 24 miles on a side, with no exurban development outside the older suburbs. Consequently, the initial densities are 7,875 persons per square mile in the city, 4,875 per square mile in the suburbs, and 5,625 per square mile in the entire metropolitan area. Moreover, all jobs are located within the city and suburbs—40 percent in the city and 60 percent in the suburbs. This situation produces an average commuting distance of 11.04 miles.

It is then assumed that a decade of population growth occurs at an average annual growth rate of 2.5 percent per year, or 28.01 percent over ten years. All this growth takes place outside the original boundaries in the exurban zone. After ten years, the area's total population has grown by 907,474 to 4.147 million, and 433,571 additional workers reside in the new exurban area. The exurbs then contain 21.9 percent of the area's total population and its total resident workers; whereas the central city and suburbs contain 27.3 percent and 50.78 percent, respectively.

Clearly, the exurbs will also have developed some job centers and will contain a significant share of all jobs. It is assumed that this share is less than the exurban share of total population; so it has been set at 10 percent, with the suburbs containing 57 percent of all jobs and the central city 33 percent. These jobs are then distributed among the area's job centers, including the new exurban ones. Some outward commuting from the city and suburbs into these centers occurs, but the flows are predominantly inward or lateral. A key question is: What impact does varying the average density of this growth have on average commuting distances (1) for the newly developing area and (2) for the metropolitan area as a whole?

If this new growth has extended evenly outward through a square 40 miles on a side, the average exurban density is very low: 886 persons per square mile. Furthermore, additional job centers have been created in the exurbs; so there are now twenty-one job centers altogether, as in the other 40-mile-square model analysis. That generates an overall average commuting distance of 13.02 miles. Substantial growth has added about 2 miles to the average commuting trip—concentrated among the new exurban workers.

The resulting commuting distances are longer than those reported for the largest U.S. metropolitan areas in *Personal Travel in the U.S.*, presented earlier. Exurbanites in particular are traveling an average of 16.44 miles to work. In contrast, if this new exurban development extends evenly only out to fill a square 30 miles on a side, its average density is 2,800 persons per square mile, or 3.2 times that in the first case above. Assuming that jobs are then shifted to only four exurban sites instead of twelve, this produces average commuting distances of 12.57 miles for all workers and 15.11 miles for exurban-resident workers. Thus, an exurban density 220 percent higher than in the 40-mile-square case produces an average exurban commuting distance of only 1.33 miles less, a drop of 8 percent. The fall in overall metropolitan area commuting distance is only 0.45 miles, or 3.5 percent.

How about even higher densities? If the same added population settles within a total area 26 miles square, exurban density rises to 9,075 persons per square mile, similar to densities in Baltimore, Washington, D.C., and Berkeley. The average density for the entire metropolitan area reaches 6,135 persons per square mile. Because the original ex-urban job centers are located outside this exurban territory, they have been moved 2 miles diagonally closer to the central business district for this computation. Also, the closer-in suburban centers described earlier—similarly 2 miles diagonally closer in—have been used in this computation. A similar calculation using the same closer-in job centers has also been made for settlement within a total area 28 miles square, which produces an average exurban density of 4,363 persons per square mile. This provides a look at a more intermediate density. Data for all four of these cases are shown in table C-3.

Thus raising exurban density from a low of 886 persons per square mile to a high of 9,075—an increase of 924 percent—lowers the average exurban commuting distance from 16.44 miles to 10.69 miles, or 35 percent. That is a considerable reduction. The average commuting distance for all metropolitan area workers falls from 13.02 miles to 9.38 miles, a decline of 28 percent.

This analysis leads to three main conclusions. First, if exurban growth occurs at medium to high average marginal densities, average commuting distances—especially for exurban residents—can be kept significantly below those that would be generated by housing the

TABLE C-3. *Commuting Distances under Four Population Density Assumptions*

	Population density			
Item	Very low	Low	Medium	High
Side of total metro area square (miles)	40	30	28	26
Was model base case modified?	Yes	No	Yes	Yes
Average exurban residents per square mile	886	2,800	4,363	9,075
Percentage increase from lowest-density case	0	216	392	924
Average miles commuting: all workers	13.02	12.57	9.49	9.38
Percentage difference from lowest-density case	0	−3.45	−27.11	−27.96
Average miles commuting: exurban workers	16.44	15.11	14.09	13.56
Percentage difference from lowest-density case	0	−8.09	−14.29	−17.52

Source: Author's calculations.

same population at very low densities. In short, residential density can make a notable difference in commuting patterns and in total commuting distances traveled per 1,000 workers. This conclusion has major implications for public policies concerning what densities should be sought in areas of new growth. It implies that low-density settlement patterns will generate a lot more commuting travel than medium-density patterns, other things being equal.

Second, it takes huge percentage changes in average densities to produce relatively small percentage changes in average commuting distances. Policies aimed at reducing travel to and from work by changing residential densities cannot be effective if they have only small or moderate impacts upon density levels.

Third, the biggest reductions in commuting distance occur when settlements are changed from very low to medium densities, rather than from medium to high densities. More than 96 percent of the decline in average commuting distance for all metropolitan area workers caused by higher-density exurban settlement results from the shift from 886 persons per square mile to 4,363 persons per square mile; less than 5 percent comes from the absolutely much larger shift from

4,363 persons to 9,075 persons. This occurs because of the inexorable laws of geometry. As the total exurban territory gets smaller, relatively tiny further shrinkages in its diameter—holding total population constant —produce big changes in average density. In contrast, when the exurban territory is much larger, absolutely large movements in its boundary have only small impacts upon its average density. This means that once a medium level of average density has been established, raising densities greatly beyond that level has relatively little impact upon average commuting distances. To put it another way, if reducing commuting distances is a goal, it is more important to avoid very low densities than to achieve very high ones.

Admittedly, the above conclusions emerge from a specific model based on very particular assumptions, but it would be possible to construct another model from different assumptions that produced quite different results. The only basic way such a model could "prove" that residential densities have no significant impact on average commuting distances would be to scatter jobs far more widely and evenly across the landscape, in relation to where people live, than this model does. I believe this model has depicted actual job location patterns with reasonable fidelity to actual conditions in large U.S. metropolitan areas, on the basis of the base-case similarity to data obtained from national travel surveys. Hence its generation of these conclusions should be considered reasonably reliable.

Appendix D

Clustering High-Density Housing near Suburban Transit Stops

O NE WAY to increase use of public transit commuting would be to cluster relatively high-density housing near suburban transit stops, especially those served by fixed-rail systems. Studies show that many who live within 2,000 feet of a rapid transit stop are willing to use public transportation for daily commuting.[1] Just how effective would this tactic be at reducing suburban traffic congestion?

A radius of 2,000 feet creates a circle containing 0.45 square miles. If 50 percent of the land within the circle contains housing, as is common in most suburban areas, 0.225 square miles of housing lies within walking distance of each transit stop. If 25 percent of the land contains housing, as in many cities, 0.11 square miles would be within walking distance. The number of such circles within a metropolitan area would depend on how many stations there were.

In the model metropolitan area analyzed in appendix C, eight outlying employment centers were located on the diagonals of the square. Assume four transit lines extended out from the downtown through these outlying centers to the corners of the 24-mile square encompassing the central city and older suburbs (but not into the newer suburbs, or exurbs). These lines would contain 68 linear route miles. Half would lie within the central city, half within the suburbs (figure D-1).

If transit stops are 0.75 miles apart in the central city, and 1.5 miles apart in the suburbs—the approximate distances in the Washington Metro system—each of the four transit lines would contain eleven stops in the city and six in the suburbs, for a total of sixty-eight. If 50 percent of the land in the suburbs was residential and 25 percent in the central city, the twenty-four suburban circles would have a

FIGURE D-1. *Model Work Trip Area Maps with Rapid Transit Lines*

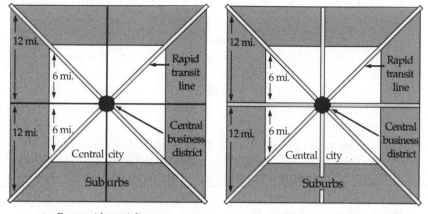

Four rapid transit lines   Eight rapid transit lines

combined net residential area of 5.4 square miles, and the forty-four city circles a combined net residential area of 4.8 square miles. These transit-oriented circles would contain 2.5 percent of all suburban residential land and 13.3 percent of all central-city residential land.

High-density, low-rise suburban housing might contain 20 units per net residential acre. If so, the 0.225 square miles of net residential land within each suburban circle would contain 2,880 dwelling units, or 7,200 people. The suburbs in this model would contain twenty-four such circles, or 172,800 people. They would comprise 10.7 percent of the total suburban population in the initial model in appendix C but a much smaller fraction (2.5 percent) of total suburban land area.

Central-city high-density housing areas might contain 50 units per net residential acre, but cover only 25 percent of gross land area. So each transit-oriented circle would include 70.4 net acres of housing holding 3,520 dwelling units, or 8,800 persons. The central city would contain forty-four circles holding 387,200 persons, 35.9 percent of the city population. In both city and suburbs combined, 560,000 persons would live in transit-oriented circles: 20.7 percent of the combined city and suburb population (excluding exurbs), and 17.2 percent of the total metropolitan area population (including exurbs).

In most U.S. central cities, densities of 50 units per net residential acre are rare. Therefore, it is more sensible to focus this analysis on suburban transit-oriented circles.

If 10.7 percent of the total suburban population lived within walking distance of transit stops, what fraction would use transit for commuting to work? That would heavily depend on how large the metropolitan area's downtown was and how much its jobs were concentrated near other transit stops. If the downtown was huge, 7–8 percent of all suburban workers might be employed there. Allowing for other jobs along the transit routes, 10 percent might be employed at locations convenient to these routes.[2] Assume that twice as many—20 percent—of those workers were employed at such locations. Even if all commuted by rapid transit, they would amount to only 2.1 percent of the total suburban working population. Thus clustering high-density housing near suburban rapid transit stops would not do much to reduce traffic congestion.

What if fixed-rail mass transit service were even more extensive? Assume there are four additional radial transit lines in this model metropolitan area. They run straight north and south or east and west from downtown to the edges of the suburban area (figure D-1). Each such line would have 6 miles of suburban routes. If it had one station every 1.5 miles, it would have four stations in the suburbs, for a total of sixteen additional suburban stations. Then the suburban total would be forty transit stops with 288,000 persons living within walking distance, 17.7 percent of the total suburban population. If even 30 percent of these worked along transit lines and all used transit for commuting, that would equal only 5.3 percent of all suburban workers.

Therefore, even extensive suburban rapid transit systems serving many high-density housing clusters near their stops would carry only relatively few suburban commuters. Creating high-density housing clusters around suburban rapid transit stops would produce minor results in comparison to the economic and political efforts required to build and maintain the transit systems and create the high-density clusters.

Notes

Introduction

1. For example, the Bay Area Council reported that 38 percent of the 630 respondents in its 1990 poll concerning pressing local issues cited traffic congestion as the area's biggest problem, compared to only 8 percent for each of the three problems ranked next. This 38 percent citation was up one-third from the 1989 poll. Congestion has been the most-cited problem for eight straight years. See Bay Area Council, *Bay Area Poll*, January 1991.

2. Kenneth A. Small, Clifford Winston, and Carol A. Evans, *Road Work: A New Highway Pricing and Investment Policy* (Brookings, 1989), p. 82.

3. James W. Hanks, Jr., and Timothy J. Lomax, *Roadway Congestion in Major Urbanized Areas, 1982 to 1988* (College Station: Texas Transportation Institute, 1990), pp. 9–24.

4. Clifford D. May, "L. I. Roads: Tie-ups Defy Solution," *New York Times*, October 7, 1986, pp. B1, B3.

5. Memorandum to the author from Robert Winick, Maryland–National Capital Park and Planning Commission, January 23, 1990.

6. Hanks and Lomax, *Roadway Congestion*, pp. xii, 48, 50.

Chapter One: Causes of Recent Increases in Traffic Congestion

1. This list corresponds to large urban areas classified as congested in a 1990 study of thirty-nine areas by the Texas Transportation Institute. Eighteen of that group were found to be congested overall in 1988; seventeen are on the list in table 1-1 (San Francisco is not, but Oakland is). Of the thirty-six areas discussed in this chapter, seventeen were classified by the study as congested overall, ten were not covered, three were incorporated into larger areas counted as congested, and only six were studied but not classified as congested. See James W. Hanks, Jr., and Timothy J. Lomax, *Roadway Congestion in Major Urbanized Areas, 1982 to 1988* (College Station: Texas Transportation Institute, 1990), p. 24.

2. Data for 1980 employment from Bureau of the Census, *State and Metropolitan Area Data Book: 1986* (Department of Commerce, 1986), p. 14; for 1990, see Salomon Brothers, *Real Estate Market Review: Supplement Edition* (January 1991), pp. 16–17.

3. Motor Vehicle Manufacturers Association, *Automobile Facts and Figures* (Detroit, various years).

4. Automobile Manufacturers' Association, *1970 Automobile Facts and Figures* (Detroit, 1970), p. 47; Motor Vehicle Manufacturers Association, *Motor Vehicle Facts and Figures '90* (Detroit, 1991), p. 44.

5. Bureau of the Census, *Statistical Abstract of the United States: 1991* (1991), p. 605; and Motor Vehicle Manufacturers Association, *Motor Vehicle Facts and Figures '90*, pp. 50, 53. The 1989 figure for total vehicle miles driven was estimated by extrapolating the rate of change from previous years.

6. Bureau of the Census, *Statistical Abstract of the United States: 1991*, p. 599.

7. Hanks and Lomax, *Roadway Congestion*, pp. C-3–C-16.

8. Federal Highway Administration, *1990 Nationwide Personal Transportation Study*, p. 17. Because total travel each day rose so sharply, it was not necessary for the degree of concentration of trips during rush hours to increase in order for such concentration to contribute to greater congestion during those hours.

9. I am indebted to Herbert Mohring of the University of Minnesota for emphasizing this underlying economic rationale for simultaneous working hours and for pointing out the socially inefficient nature of current practices. One tactic for reducing congestion analyzed later is staggering working hours. But even when work starting times are staggered, most work hours overlap with those of other workers so that the interorganizational efficiency of simultaneity can be retained.

10. Federal Highway Administration, *Personal Travel in the U.S.*, vol. 1: *1983–1984 Nationwide Personal Transportation Study* (Department of Transportation, 1986), p. 6-28.

11. Computed from Department of Transportation, *Transportation Planning Data for Urbanized Areas Based on the 1980 Census* (1985), chaps. 1, 2.

12. Federal Highway Administration, *1990 Nationwide Personal Transportation Study*, p. 9.

13. William M. Rohe and others, *Travel to Work Patterns: A Preliminary Analysis of Selected Data from the Annual Housing Survey Travel-to-Work File* (University of North Carolina, Department of City and Regional Planning, 1980), p. 145.

14. William P. O'Hare and Milton Morris, *Demographic Change and Recent Worktrip Travel Trends*, vol. 1: *Final Report* (Washington: Joint Center for Political Studies, 1985), p. 104

15. See Peter Gordon, Harry Richardson, and Genevieve Giuliano, *Travel Trends in Non-CBD Activity Centers* (University of Southern California, School of Urban and Regional Planning, 1989), p. 16.

16. Coldwell Banker Commercial Toro Wheaton Services, *Coldwell Banker Commercial Office Vacancy Index of the United States, December 31, 1989* (Boston,

1990), p. 1. This publication does not list (or apparently, track) office space within central cities but outside downtown markets.

17. In some areas and under some circumstances driving alone may take more time and be less convenient than ride sharing or using public transit. But on average this is not the case. In 1983 average commuting times were 19.1 minutes for persons using private passenger cars, 20.1 minutes for those using trucks, vans, and other private vehicles, and 46.1 minutes for those using public transportation. Average speeds were 31.1 miles per hour for the first group, 33.7 for the second, and 19.7 for the third. Federal Highway Administration, *Personal Travel in the U.S.*, vol. 1, p. 7-9.

18. See Federal Highway Administration, *Personal Travel in the U.S.*, vol. 1, p. 7-19. In 1977, 72.0 percent of all morning peak-period commuters were private vehicle drivers and 18.3 percent were passengers, while the average car pool then held 1.52 passengers. By 1983 these figures had changed to 76.7 percent, 11.8 percent, and 1.49 respectively.

19. Charles Lave, *Things Won't Get a Lot Worse: The Future of U.S. Traffic Congestion* (University of California at Irvine, Institute of Transportation Studies and Department of Economics, 1990).

20. Southern California Association of Governments, *Regional Mobility Plan* (February 1989), p. III-1.

21. Federal Highway Administration, *1990 Nationwide Personal Transportation Study*, pp. 19, 37.

22. In 1988, households with 1987 incomes less than $10,000 owned an average of 1.3 vehicles; those with incomes of $25,000 to $34,000 owned 1.8; and those with incomes of $35,000 to $49,999 owned 2.2. Motor Vehicle Manufacturers Association, *Motor Vehicle Facts and Figures '90*, p. 45.

Chapter Two: Strategies for Reducing Congestion and Four Traffic Principles

1. This distinction has been developed by the Bay Area Economic Forum in a series of three documents entitled *Market-Based Solutions to the Transportation Crisis* (San Francisco, 1990).

2. Bay Area Economic Forum, *Market-Based Solutions to the Transportation Crisis: The Concept*, p. 7.

3. See Federal Highway Administration, *Personal Travel in the U.S.:* vol. 1, *1983–1984 Nationwide Personal Transportation Study* (Department of Transportation, 1986), p. 7-13.

4. See Federal Highway Administration, *Personal Travel in the U.S.*, vol. 1, pp. 4-4, 7-13.

5. Kenneth Small, University of California, Irvine, and Clifford Winston of Brookings pointed out this possibility.

6. For further discussion of the idea of convergence, see Anthony Downs, "The Law of Peak-Hour Expressway Congestion," *Traffic Quarterly*, vol. 16 (July 1962), pp. 393–409.

7. Kenneth Small and Frederick Ducca of the Bureau of Public Roads pointed out that modal convergence also takes place.

8. Frederick Ducca pointed out this possibility.

9. However, if such a public transit improvement occurs, there would not be a net increase in highway usage from modal convergence. Rather, improved public transit would cause a net shift away from the road system to the public transit system. The other two forms of convergence would still take place.

10. This point was made by Richard Tustian (planning director of Montgomery County in suburban Washington, D.C., during the 1970s and 1980s) in his extremely helpful comments on the original draft of this book.

11. It is true that much of the interstate highway system was built long after massive movements to the suburbs began. But any observer of how new housing and commercial real estate developments sprout along new roadways cannot help but conclude that roadways have influenced at least the location of such growth, if not its total amount.

12. In many metropolitan areas, this principle applies to the central city as well as to its suburbs. But some central cities contain such large fractions of the jobs and population of the metropolitan area that local policies might influence the growth prospects for the area as a whole.

13. As Kenneth Small has pointed out, more commuters may travel during periods of maximum convenience both because travel capacity during those periods has risen and because the definition of such periods has changed as a result of altered traffic conditions.

Chapter Three: Increasing Carrying Capacity

1. In 1980 there were 139.83 million cars and trucks in use and 226.55 million residents in the United States, or 61.7 vehicles per 100 residents. By 1989, there were 175.96 million such vehicles and 248.26 million residents, or 70.9 vehicles per 100 residents. See Motor Vehicle Manufacturers Association, *Motor Vehicle Facts and Figures '90* (Detroit, 1990), pp. 28-29; and Bureau of the Census, *Statistical Abstract of the United States: 1990* (1991), p. 7.

2. See Anthony Downs, "The Law of Peak-Hour Expressway Congestion," *Traffic Quarterly*, vol. 16 (July 1962), pp. 393-409.

3. For more details, see Urban Land Institute, Growth Problems Task Force, "Transportation and Growth: Eight Steps to Managing Congestion" (September 10, 1990).

4. Washington State Department of Transportation, *FLOW—A Two Year Evaluation* (Seattle, 1983), p. 11.

5. Washington State Department of Transportation, *Six-Year FLOW Evaluation* (Seattle, 1989), pp. 3, 14.

6. This calculation does not take into account the fixed costs of vehicle ownership; rather, it assumes the commuter would own a car no matter how he or she was traveling to and from work. Operating costs are 10 cents per

mile on a commuting trip of 9 miles each way. This method of calculation was suggested by Herbert Mohring.

7. If one-fourth of an hour is worth $4.80, a full hour is worth four times as much, or $19.20. Note, too, that free parking strongly encourages commuters to drive alone. If the commuter enjoys free parking, it is 20 cents less expensive to drive alone than to travel by bus and takes less time. The commuter would then be motivated to drive alone unless bus travel or ride sharing took less time than solo driving. That is quite unlikely unless peak-hour congestion in the area is horrendous and HOV lanes are extremely effective at avoiding it.

8. See John R. Meyer and Jose A. Gomez-Ibanez, *Autos, Transit, and Cities* (Harvard University Press, 1981). Diverting existing lanes to HOV use can raise total capacity under some conditions. For example, if 200 vehicles save 10 minutes each on the HOV lane, and each carries an average of 2.5 persons, then 5,000 person-minutes are saved. If this causes 1,000 vehicles with solo drivers to lose 2 minutes apiece, they lose 2,000 person-minutes. Hence there is a net gain to society of 3,000 person-minutes. This example was furnished by Kenneth Small. But he did not point out that this exchange is a political loser. Five hundred people feel better because they saved 10 minutes each, but 1,000 people are angry because they not only lost 2 minutes each but also saw other people whizzing by on lanes they formerly used themselves. In a democracy, 1,000 votes outweigh 500—especially when the 1,000 have more intense emotions about the issue than the 500.

9. This suggestion was made by Herbert Mohring.

10. See Morgan State University, Center for Transportation Studies, *A Study to Assess the Importance of Personal, Social, Psychological and Other Factors in Ridesharing Programs* (Department of Transportation, 1984), pp. 66-67, 84. From surveys of ride-sharing commuters, this report concluded that "94 percent of the males and 84 percent of the females both suggested that economic factors influence their decisions on joining ridesharing programs" (p. 66). This survey showed that 73.7 percent of male respondents and 71.5 percent of female respondents cited economic factors as "very important" in this decision, followed by "personal" reasons (p. 67). Similar conclusions were reached by the National Capital Region Transportation Planning Board, *1987 Survey and Evaluation of Ride Finders Ridesharing Network* (Washington: Metropolitan Council of Governments, 1987).

11. Federal Highway Administration, *Personal Travel in the U.S.*, vol. 1: *1983–1984 Nationwide Personal Transportation Study* (Department of Transportation, 1986), p. 7-11.

12. C. Kenneth Orski, "Emerging Responses to the New Transportation Environment: A National Overview," in *Mobility for Major Metropolitan Growth Centers: A New Challenge for Public-Private Cooperation* (University of California, Irvine, Institute of Transportation Studies, and University of California, Los Angeles, Public Policy Program, 1985), p. 12.

13. Bay Area Economic Forum, *Market-Based Solutions to the Transportation Crisis: The Concept* (San Francisco, 1990), p. 5.

14. William P. O'Hare and Milton Morris, *Demographic Change and Recent Worktrip Travel Trends*, vol. 1: *Final Report* (Washington: Joint Center for Political Studies, 1985), pp. 30, 104.

15. O'Hare and Morris, *Demographic Change*, vol. 1, pp. 30, 104.

16. Earlier in this chapter, it was assumed that total downtown employment in the 1980s grew at the same rate as employment nationwide. This is consistent with a declining share of downtown employment among all urbanized area jobs because the latter grew faster than employment nationwide, owing to slower job growth outside metropolitan areas.

17. Boris S. Pushkarev and Jeffrey M. Zupan, *Public Transportation and Land Use Policy* (Indiana University Press, 1977), pp. 172–73.

18. BART could haul more passengers during both peak and off-peak periods. BART's total traffic reached 61.4 million passengers in 1985 but dropped by 5.1 million when fares were increased in 1986. Annual traffic remained below 59 million until the earthquake raised it to 65.9 million in 1989. So the failure of BART traffic to grow larger should not be attributed to its having reached the physical limits of the current system's carrying capacity. Telephone conversation with Joan Demurra of BART, November 14, 1990; and *Bay Area Rapid Transit District Annual Report, 1988/1989*. There were 1.892 million workers in these areas in 1990, a gain of 9.9 percent over the 1985 level.

19. Salomon Brothers, *Real Estate Market Review, October 1990*, p. 27. The employment total used here differs slightly from that used in chapter 8 because the two come from different sources. However, there is no significant difference in their implications as used in this analysis. Data on Metro ridership were obtained from John F. Fularz in the Washington Metropolitan Area Transit Authority Office of Planning. These estimates assume that 40 percent of all Metro trips consist of persons traveling to (but not from) work. That assumption is based on a survey of Metro rail riders taken in 1990, also supplied by Fularz. Approximately 2.264 million workers were employed in this entire area in 1990.

20. As John Meyer has pointed out, this would not necessarily have occurred if the same money spent on Metro had been spent improving highways and bus services and on creating limited-access bus lanes in the Washington metropolitan area.

21. Author's calculation from data in Salomon Brothers, *Real Estate Market Review, January 1991*, p. 17.

Chapter Four: Peak-Hour Road Pricing

1. William S. Vickrey and Herbert Mohring are among the pioneers in devising analyses that indicate a need for peak-hour road pricing in order to achieve economic efficiency. See William S. Vickrey, "Some Implications of Marginal Cost Pricing for Public Utilities," *American Economic Review, Papers*

and Proceedings, vol. 45 (1955), pp. 605–20; and Vickrey, "General and Specific Financing of Urban Services," in Howard G. Schaller, ed., *Public Expenditure Decisions in the Urban Community* (Washington: Resources for the Future, 1963), pp. 62–90. Herbert Mohring, "Urban Highway Investments," in Robert Dorfman, ed., *Measuring Benefits of Government Investment* (Brookings, 1965), pp. 231–75; and Mohring, "The Peak-Load Problem with Increasing Returns and Pricing Constraints," *American Economic Review*, vol. 60 (1970), pp. 693–705. A brief bibliography of more recent articles on peak-hour road pricing can be found in Kenneth A. Small, Clifford Winston, and Carol A. Evans, *Road Work: A New Highway Pricing and Investment Policy* (Brookings, 1989), p. 87, notes 16–19.

2. In this discussion, *collective costs* are those experienced by an entire group, as opposed to *individual costs*. Where the time losses are caused by traffic congestion, both collective and individual losses are *private costs*, experienced by individuals as such, rather than *social costs* experienced by society as a whole, including groups and individuals. Hence *collective costs* can be either private or social, whereas individual costs are always private. The capital costs of building more road capacity because of congestion are *social costs* if they are borne by society as a whole through general government expenditures.

3. Bay Area Economic Forum, *Market-Based Solutions to the Transportation Crisis: The Concept* (San Francisco, 1990), p. 7.

4. Clifford Winston pointed out this distinction.

5. Tim Hau of the World Bank provided current information about which cities have adopted partial road pricing and which are considering broader systems.

6. Motor Vehicle Manufacturers Association, *Motor Vehicle Facts and Figures '89* (Detroit, 1989), p. 46.

7. C. Kenneth Orski, "Congestion Pricing: Promise and Limitations," remarks presented at the 1991 National Planning Conference, New Orleans, p. 8.

8. Small, Winston, and Evans, *Road Work*, p. 98.

9. Kenneth A. Small, "The Incidence of Congestion Tolls on Urban Highways," *Journal of Urban Economics*, vol. 13 (January 1983), pp. 90–111.

10. Letter from Herbert Mohring, May 12, 1991: "Plowing congestion tolls back into road improvements is not necessarily efficient. Presume zero population and travel growth, infinitely durable roads, and an optimally designed road network. Marginal-cost tolls would then function as a normal return on the resources that society has invested in its road network. Efficiency would dictate using road-user tolls just as any other source of government revenues. Efficiency would not dictate spending these revenues on road improvements."

11. The technology is described in detail in Ian Catling and Brian J. Harbord, "Electronic Road-Pricing in Hong Kong: 2. The Technology," *Traffic Engineering + Control* (December 1985), pp. 608–15.

12. Tim Hau provided this information about why the Hong Kong experiment was not extended into a permanent system.

13. Two analyses that have been done are Anthony Gomez-Ibanez and Gary R. Fauth, *Journal of Transport Economics and Policy*, vol. 14 (1980), pp. 133–53; and Marvin Kraus, "The Welfare Gains from Pricing Road Congestion Using Automatic Vehicle Identification and On-Vehicle Meters," *Journal of Urban Economics*, vol. 25 (1989), pp. 261–81.

14. The Los Angeles Airport is now using an automatic vehicle identification system with ENP devices to reduce commercial van and truck congestion. Many such vehicles are charged varying tolls for entering and remaining on the airport's main drives. The longer they stay within a designated and heavily congested area, the higher the charges they incur.

15. This possibility was suggested by Clifford Winston.

16. Urban Institute and KT Analytics, *Proposal to Conduct a Congestion Pricing Study*, prepared for the Southern California Association of Governments, June 18, 1990, p. 17.

17. Kenneth A. Small suggested this point.

18. Small, Winston, and Evans, *Road Work*, p. 95.

19. Calvin Sims, "No-Stop Tolls: 3 States Agree to Automation," *New York Times*, April 4, 1991, pp. A1, B4.

20. Information obtained from Kenneth A. Small.

21. Small, Winston, and Evans, *Road Work*, p. 97.

22. See Orski, "Congestion Pricing."

Chapter Five: Demand-Side Remedies that Focus on Behavior

1. Federal Highway Administration, *Personal Travel in the U.S.*, vol. 1: *1983–1984 Nationwide Personal Transportation Study* (Department of Transportation, 1986), pp. 6-26, 6-28.

2. Federal Highway Administration, *Personal Travel in the U.S.*, vol. 1, p. 7-9.

3. Robert T. Dunphy and Ben C. Lin, *Transportation Management through Partnerships* (Washington: Urban Land Institute, 1990), pp. 159–60.

4. See COMSIS Corporation, *Evaluation of Travel Demand Management Measures to Relieve Congestion* (Federal Highway Administration, February 1990).

5. See COMSIS, *Evaluation*.

6. In 1987 the average spending on transportation, as a fraction of average income before taxes, was 33.6 percent for households in the lowest 20 percent of the income distribution, 19.8 percent in the middle 20 percent, and 12.7 percent in the highest 20 percent. Bureau of the Census, *Statistical Abstract of the United States: 1990* (1991), pp. 442–43.

7. Bureau of the Census, *Statistical Abstract of the United States: 1989* (1989), p. 481.

8. Data obtained by telephone from the American Petroleum Institute.

9. The *price elasticity* of any product is the percentage by which the quantity

of that product purchased would decline for each 1 percent rise in its price. Charles River Associates, *Price Elasticities of Demand for Transportation Fuels* (Cambridge, Mass., 1976).

10. This calculation assumes the "point" elasticity estimate would remain valid over a large range of change.

11. John Pucher, "Urban Travel Behavior as the Outcome of Public Policy: The Example of Modal-Split in Western Europe and North America," *American Planning Association Journal* (Autumn 1988), pp. 509–19.

12. Richard Wilson and Donald Shoup, "Parking Subsidies and Travel Choices: Assessing the Evidence," *Transportation*, vol. 17 (1990), p. 144.

13. Bay Area Economic Forum, *Market-Based Solutions to the Transportation Crisis: Executive Summary* (San Francisco, 1990).

14. See Federal Highway Deputy Administrator Eugene R. McCormick, "An Update on the Federal IVHS Program," statement prepared for the 1992 annual meeting of the Transportation Research Board, p. 5.

15. For an overview of IHVS, see Federal Highway Administration, *An Overview of the IVHS Program through FY 1991* (October 1991). Much of the information in this section was taken from this publication and from others supplied by H. Milton Heywood of the Federal Highway Administration.

16. For a scathing but accurate critique of IVHS, see Clifford Winston, "Building a Better Traffic Jam," *New York Times*, December 21, 1991, p. 19. Winston believes most of the money allocated to IVHS would be better spent on implementing peak-hour road pricing systems.

Chapter Six: Remedies That Increase Residential Densities

1. A detailed discussion of these two measures of residential density and their relationship is presented in appendix B.

2. Real Estate Research Corporation, *The Costs of Sprawl. Detailed Cost Analysis* (Washington, April 1974).

3. Cross-commuting occurs when most people who live near job site A work at other sites—say, B through F—quite distant from their homes and from site A; whereas most people who reside close to job sites B through F work in other job sites quite distant from their homes—including site A. Cross-commuting workers choose job and home locations that generate much longer-than-minimal commuting journeys. Consequently, many such commuters pass each other going to and from their homes and jobs each day.

4. Boris S. Pushkarev and Jeffrey M. Zupan, *Public Transportation and Land Use Policy* (Indiana University Press, 1977).

5. Concerning age, the higher the proportion of working adults as opposed to either children or the elderly, the higher the area's incidence of automobile ownership, and therefore the lower the propensity of its residents to use public transit.

6. The availability of commuter rail tends to increase the usage of public transit.

7. Pushkarev and Zupan, *Public Transportation*, p. 177.

8. Computed as 7 units per acre times 2.5 persons per unit times 320 acres. If only 30 percent of the land is used for housing, the gross density figure could be as low as 3,360 persons per square mile. But if 70 percent of the land is in housing, that figure would be 7,840 persons per square mile.

9. Pushkarev and Zupan, *Public Transportation*, pp. 5, 177.

10. See Gary Delsohn, "The First Pedestrian Pocket," *Planning Magazine*, vol. 55 (December 1989), pp. 20–22.

11. Frederick Ducca pointed out this relationship.

12. The residential densities used in this analysis are computed with 1989 population and area data for individual incorporated communities. These are gross residential densities—that is, residents per square mile, including all land within each community in the base of square miles counted. All the residents of each community are counted as living at the average density for that community. The distribution of all residents within the metropolitan area is calculated by adding up the total number of residents living there in each of seven density ranges, from less than 2,500 persons per square mile to 10,000 or more. These densities are not calculated for the entire geographic area encompassed by each metropolitan area, but only for those communities in its urbanized portions. This approach excludes large uninhabited or thinly settled areas from the calculations.

13. These comparisons are somewhat misleading because Los Angeles County contains only the oldest and closest-in of the suburbs of Los Angeles City. Its newer suburbs extend into Orange, Riverside, San Bernardino, and Ventura counties as well. The data given here for the suburbs of both Chicago and New York City include all such suburbs within their respective states, not just the older, closer-in suburbs. For example, all Long Island communities have been counted as suburbs of New York City, even though they form a separate metropolitan area in Census Bureau statistics.

14. See Advisory Commission on Regulatory Barriers to Affordable Housing, *"Not In My Back Yard: Removing Barriers to Affordable Housing"* (Washington, 1991).

15. A LULU is a "locally undesirable land use." It produces great benefits for its entire region, but negative spillover effects on those living near it. Examples are airports, expressways, and trash incinerators. NIMBY stands for "not in my back yard." A NIMBY attitude means opposing location of any LULU near one's own home, even though one recognizes it ought to be built somewhere. Since residents near any site proposed for a LULU almost always adopt a NIMBY attitude toward it, choosing sites for LULUs becomes extremely difficult.

16. This subject is analyzed in more depth in chapter 9. The Advisory Commission on Regulatory Barriers to Affordable Housing also concluded that existing exclusionary land-use policies adopted by local governments

could best be changed through state governments' adopting statewide regulations requiring reexamination and alteration of such policies. See the commission's *"Not In My Back Yard,"* pp. 7-1–7-15, 13-16.

17. Urban growth boundaries also raise land prices within the boundaries faster than they would otherwise rise and keep land prices outside the boundaries from rising as fast as they otherwise would. For a discussion of their nature and effects, see Gerrit J. Knaap and Arthur C. Nelson, "The Effects of Regional Land Use Control in Oregon: A Theoretical and Empirical Review," *Review of Regional Studies,* vol. 18 (Spring 1988), pp. 37–46.

18. For a discussion of this issue, see Richard B. Peiser, "Density and Urban Sprawl," *Land Economics,* vol. 65 (August 1989), pp. 193–204.

19. See Advisory Commission on Regulatory Barriers to Affordable Housing, *"Not In My Back Yard,"* p. 8-2. The fifteen studies are listed in note 1 on p. 8-11. The Urban Land Institute has developed a video presentation explaining how developers can create relatively high-density multifamily housing that is aesthetically attractive and an asset to its community.

Chapter Seven: Changing the Jobs-Housing Balance

1. A description of jobs-housing imbalances, how they arise, and their negative effects is presented by Robert Cervero in "Jobs-Housing Balancing and Regional Mobility," *American Planning Association Journal,* vol. 55 (1989), pp. 136–50; reprinted in Lincoln Institute for Land Policy, *Achieving a Jobs-Housing Balance: Land Use Planning for Regional Growth, Resource Manual 1991* (Cambridge, Mass., 1991), sec. 2.2.

2. Cervero, "Jobs-Housing Balancing," p. 137.

3. Arnold Sherwood, "Job/Housing Balance," in Lincoln Institute for Land Policy, *Achieving a Jobs-Housing Balance,* sec. 2.5. The "targets" adopted by SCAG were to shift 9 percent of all new jobs into areas with a housing surplus and 5 percent of all new housing into areas with a job surplus. See Martin Nachs, "Thought Piece on the Jobs/Housing Balance," in Lincoln Institute for Land Policy, *Achieving a Jobs-Housing Balance,* sec. 2.4.

4. Genevieve Giuliano, "Is Jobs Housing Balance a Transportation Issue?" in Lincoln Institute for Land Policy, *Achieving a Jobs-Housing Balance,* sec. 2.1.

5. Peter Gordon, Harry Richardson, and Myung-Jin Jun, "The Commuting Paradox: Evidence from the Top Twenty," in Lincoln Institute for Land Policy, *Achieving a Jobs-Housing Balance,* sec. 2.3.

6. Bureau of the Census, *Statistical Abstract of the United States: 1990* (1990), pp. 442–43.

7. See Giuliano, "Is Jobs-Housing Balance a Transportation Issue?"

8. Traveling 10 miles in twenty minutes implies an average speed of 30 miles per hour. The actual average speed of automotive vehicle commuters in

1983 was 31.1 miles per hour, according to Federal Highway Administration, *Personal Travel in the U.S.*, vol. 1: *1983–1984 Nationwide Personal Transportation Study* (Department of Transportation, 1986), p. 7-9. The average hourly wage in the United States for all private nonagricultural production workers in 1988 was $9.29, according to Bureau of the Census, *Statistical Abstract of the United States: 1990*, p. 402.

9. See Cervero, "Jobs-Housing Balancing," pp. 139–40

10. Robert B. Zehner, *Access, Travel, and Transportation in New Communities* (Cambridge, Mass.: Ballinger, 1977).

11. Cervero, "Jobs-Housing Balancing," p. 138.

12. Hamilton, Rabinovitz, and Alschuler, "Thinking about Jobs-Housing Balance in Los Angeles," in Lincoln Institute for Land Policy, *Achieving a Jobs-Housing Balance*, sec. 3.3.

13. Housing price data from the National Association of Realtors for the San Francisco Bay area.

14. This is evident from the policies recommended by Cervero. He suggested considering requiring homebuilders to include a certain fraction of units for low- and moderate-income households in every housing project, granting federal tax credits and federally tax exempt municipal bond financing to developers of multifamily housing for moderate-income households, and allowing higher densities of offices to commercial developers who create nearby housing. He also proposed requiring developers of commercial properties to contribute money to housing trust funds or to build nearby housing units, adopting tax-base sharing throughout a metropolitan area, having the state government require every local community to adopt a fair-share target for low- and moderate-income units, and raising the cost of driving through higher gasoline taxes, highway tolls, and parking fees, or all four. See Cervero, "Jobs-Housing Balancing," p. 140; and Cervero, "Jobs/Housing Balance as Public Policy," *Urban Land* (October 1991), pp. 10–14

15. Bureau of the Census, *Statistical Abstract of the United States: 1990*, pp. 19, 721.

16. For example, Genevieve Giuliano showed that the ratio of resident workers to local jobs had risen from 1974 to 1988 in Riverside, San Bernardino, and Ventura counties in the Los Angeles area—all areas with a housing surplus. In contrast, it had fallen in Los Angeles and Orange counties during the same period. Giuliano, "Is Jobs-Housing Balance a Transportation Issue?" p. 7.

17. This conclusion differs from the conclusion about "spontaneous" trends drawn by Giuliano in her analysis of jobs-housing balance strategies. I believe she did not take sufficient account of qualitative imbalances in her analysis. However, her ultimate conclusion about the wisdom of trying to reduce traffic congestion by changing jobs-housing balances is the same as mine. See "Is Jobs-Housing Balance a Transportation Issue?"

18. See Larry P. Arnn, "Jobs-Housing Balance: Too Good to Be True; Too Easy to Be Good—Some Lessons for the Inland Empire," *Golden State Briefings* (Montclair, Calif.: Claremont Institute, 1990).

19. Giuliano, "Is Jobs-Housing Balance a Transportation Issue?" pp. 14–15.

20. William P. O'Hare and Milton Morris, *Demographic Change and Recent Worktrip Travel Trends*, vol. 2: *Statistical Tables* (Washington: Joint Center for Political Studies, 1985), table I-80.

Chapter Eight: Concentrating Jobs in Large Clusters

1. IBI Group in association with various consultants, *Summary Report: Greater Toronto Area Urban Structure Concepts Study* (Greater Toronto Coordinating Committee, June 1990). As John Meyer pointed out to me, the three alternatives proposed in this report really form three points along a continuous spectrum of possible arrangements. Hence many other combinations along this spectrum are also possible.

2. Peter Gordon, Harry Richardson, and Genevieve Giuliano, *Travel Trends in Non-CBD Activity Centers* (University of Southern California, School of Urban and Regional Planning, 1989), p. 16.

3. The term *edge city* was coined by Joel Garreau, *Edge Cities: Life on the New Frontier* (Macmillan, 1991), p. 4.

4. Federal Highway Administration, *Personal Travel in the U.S.*, vol. 1: *1983–1984 Nationwide Personal Transportation Study* (Department of Transportation, 1986), p. 7-11. The proportion of all workers who commuted by private vehicles was 89.7 percent in 1977 and 87.4 percent in 1983. Among central city resident workers, this proportion was 84.7 percent in 1977 and 81.7 percent in 1983. Hence suburban-resident workers are only slightly more likely to drive to work than all other types of workers.

5. C. Kenneth Orski, "Evaluating Travel Demand Management Effectiveness," Washington: Urban Mobility Corp., 1991, table 2.

6. Some bus systems in less developed nations operate profitably. So do a few fixed-rail systems, such as those in Hong Kong and Singapore. But these are exceptional.

7. In theory, a large city could try to consolidate scattered jobs into one or more clusters within its boundaries without having to deal with any regionwide agency or other governments. But the job-concentration strategy would work best when applied to areas of new growth. Most big cities are almost entirely settled, except for a few that still contain some vacant land, such as San Diego. Moreover, the shopping centers and related clusters within their boundaries already have a higher internal density than the suburban center discussed in the next section of this chapter. Hence this strategy probably will not work well within most large cities

Chapter Nine: Local Growth-Management Policies

1. The literature on growth management and growth-management laws is too vast to cite extensively here. Hence only a few citations will be made to highly relevant portions.

2. See Robert Cervero, *Suburban Gridlock* (Center for Urban Policy Research of Rutgers University, 1986); Madelyn Glickfeld and Ned Levine, *The New Land Use Regulation "Revolution": Why California's Local Jurisdictions Enact Growth Control and Management Measures* (University of California at Los Angeles Extension Public Policy Program, June 22, 1990); and Elizabeth Deakin, "Land Use and Transportation Planning in Response to Congestion: A Review and Critique," paper prepared for the 1989 annual meeting of the Transportation Research Board.

3. See Glickfeld and Levine, *New Land Use Regulation "Revolution."*

4. See Seymour I. Schwartz, David E. Hansen, and Richard D. Green, "Suburban Growth Controls and the Price of New Housing," *Journal of Environmental Economics and Management*, vol. 8 (December 1981), pp. 303–20; and Lawrence Katz and Kenneth T. Rosen, "The Interjurisdictional Effects of Growth Controls on Housing Prices," *Journal of Law and Economics*, vol. 30 (April 1987), pp. 149–60.

5. This point was taken in part from the analysis of growth management policies carried out by William Fischel. See "What Do Economists Know about Growth Controls? A Research Review," in David J. Brower, David R. Godschalk, and Douglas R. Porter, eds., *Understanding Growth Management: Critical Issues and a Research Agenda* (Washington: Urban Land Institute, 1989), pp. 59–86.

6. Or perhaps *because of* higher prices, since the higher prices are a sign of greater exclusivity.

Chapter Ten: The Need for Regional Anticongestion Policies

1. Raising gasoline taxes would be most effective if done by the federal government, rather than state governments, because many metropolitan areas contain parts of more than one state, or are quite close to another state. If one of the states increased its gasoline taxes but one or more of the others did not, motorists would patronize the ones that did not. That would vitiate the impact of the tax increase and injure gasoline outlets in the state that raised taxes. Among the metropolitan areas or consolidated regions that cross state lines are New York City, Boston, Philadelphia, Chicago, Minneapolis–St. Paul, St. Louis, Portland (Oregon), Washington, D.C., Cincinnati, and Providence. States in which major population centers are relatively distant from neighboring states could successfully avoid this problem. Probably the most important among these states are California, Florida, and Texas, in which more than one-half of all U.S. population growth has occurred since 1970.

2. Some parts of the interstate highway system do charge tolls. They are mainly portions incorporated into the system from preexisting toll roads. Examples are the Pennsylvania Toll Road, the Ohio Toll Road, the toll road system around Chicago, and interstate 95 through Delaware. However, the

federal government does not now permit placing tolls on any additional portions of the interstate system.

3. For a study of bureaucratic resistance to change, see Anthony Downs, *Inside Bureaucracy* (Little, Brown, 1967).

4. Alexis de Tocqueville, *Democracy in America*, vol. 1 (Knopf, 1972), p. 198. This tendency was more recently celebrated in Robert N. Bellah and others, *Habits of the Heart: Individualism and Commitment in American Life* (Harper and Row, 1985).

5. For a detailed analysis of how this arrangement works in a democracy and why it is an advantage of democracies over other systems, see Anthony Downs, *An Economic Theory of Democracy* (Harper and Row, 1957).

6. See Anthony Downs, "Up and Down with Ecology: The Issue-Attention Cycle," in David L. Protess and Maxwell McCombs, eds., *Agenda Setting: Readings on Media, Public Opinion, and Policymaking* (Hillsdale, N.J.: Lawrence Erlbaum Associates, 1991), pp. 27–33.

Chapter Eleven: Summary and Conclusions

1. This estimate was derived from Federal Highway Administration, *Personal Travel in the U.S.*, vol. 1: *1983–1984 Nationwide Personal Transportation Study* (Department of Transportation, 1986), pp. 7-19, 7-23.

2. In theory, extensive adoption of either peak-hour road pricing or peak-hour long-term parking surcharges within a metropolitan area could substantially reduce peak-hour traffic congestion without the use of other tactics, as discussed further later. But neither is likely to be adopted on a sufficient scale to accomplish that goal at one stroke.

3. Federal Highway Administration, *Personal Travel in the U.S.*, vol. 1, pp. 6-28, 7-19; and author's calculations with data from chapter 2.

4. Congress structured inheritance taxes so that no state can gain a competitive advantage over other states by failing to pass a state inheritance tax. If a state does not pass such a tax, the federal government will collect the same revenues from its citizens as state governments that have inheritance taxes are collecting from their citizens. Thus the citizens of states without such taxes have no advantage, the state governments gain no revenues, and every state has a strong incentive to adopt the type of inheritance tax promoted by Congress.

Appendix A

1. This appendix has benefited greatly from comments on an earlier draft by Kenneth A. Small, Herbert Mohring, and Clifford Winston.

2. This diagram is a version of a well-known set of relationships that has appeared in many previous analyses of this subject. For a recent and more elaborate version, see Timothy D. Hau, "An Economic Analysis of Road

Pricing: A Diagrammatic Approach," preliminary draft, World Bank, April 19, 1991. Timothy Hau provided information on road pricing systems throughout the world.

Appendix B

1. Boris S. Pushkarev and Jeffrey M. Zupan, *Public Transportation and Land Use Policy* (Indiana University Press, 1977), exhibit 7.2.

2. Note that 69,333 divided by 2.0 persons per dwelling equals 34,666 dwellings per square mile. If there are 210.6 dwellings per net acre, those 34,666 dwellings occupy 164.6 acres. That is 25.7 percent of the 640 acres in the 1 square mile containing the 69,333 persons.

3. Pushkarev and Zupan, *Public Transportation*, p. 202, present a conversion chart for relating gross population per square mile to dwelling units per residential acre.

Net dwellings per acre	Population per gross square mile
2	1,730
5	3,410
7	1,812
10	2,485
20	4,725
30	6,965
50	11,445
100	22,645

Assuming an average household size of 2.5 persons, these data imply that the percentage of land devoted to residential use varies from a high of 54 percent at 2 dwellings per acre to a low of 35 percent at 100 dwellings per acre.

Appendix C

1. Concentrating all jobs in these thirteen nodes greatly simplifies the calculation of average travel distances from each of the 1,600 square miles in this model. Because there are thirteen such centers, five in the city, four in the older suburbs, and four in the exurbs, jobs can still be spread widely across the entire map while remaining within these centers. Hence this simplification does not distort reality significantly, even though real-world jobs are much more widely scattered across the landscape.

2. This distance can be measured either *rectangularly* (assuming all movements are either purely vertical or purely horizontal) or *diagonally* (assuming

all movements are in straight lines directly connecting the center of each residential square mile with each job center). Because actual street patterns combine both rectangular and diagonal elements, the average of these two distances has been used to represent the average commuting distance between each square mile and each job center.

3. The commuting distances for a large U.S. metropolitan area shown in this table have been taken from Federal Highway Administration, *Personal Travel in the U.S.*, vol. 1: *1983–1984 Nationwide Personal Transportation Study* (Department of Transportation, 1986), pp. 7-3, 7-5. The metropolitan average commuting distance shown is from 1983 for areas containing 3 million or more residents (p. 7-5). However, that source contained no breakouts for suburbs or the central city. Hence the average commuting distances for exurbs and suburbs combined (similar to the Department of Transportation's category "not in a central city") and for the central city have been extrapolated to large metropolitan areas from data concerning *all* metropolitan areas (p. 7-3). These extrapolations are marked with a superscript b in table C-1.

4. William P. O'Hare and Milton Morris, *Demographic Change and Recent Worktrip Travel Trends*, vol. 2: *Statistical Tables* (Washington: Joint Center for Political Studies, 1985), table I-80. The average travel time for all metropolitan area workers was 22.2 minutes. The lowest time was 18.8 minutes for workers living and working in the suburbs, and 20.0 minutes for those living and working in central cities (p. 104). The model shows shorter distances for the latter than the former. However, these data could be consistent with the model's seemingly opposite results because 30.2 percent of all city-resident workers who have city jobs use public transit to commute, compared with 2.6 percent of all suburban-resident workers who have suburban jobs. But commuting by public transit is much slower than commuting by car; hence suburban workers could have longer trips in space but shorter ones in time.

5. This outcome can be changed by shifting percentages of jobs among specific job centers so as to make the 24-mile-square average distance either slightly larger than, the same as, or slightly smaller than the 30-mile-square average distance. The basic implication is that there is not much difference between these two cases.

6. As indicated above, 68 percent of this fall in commuting distance was caused by higher density and 32 percent by moving the suburban job centers closer to the downtown—thereby making them more central to the reduced suburban residential area.

Appendix D

1. See Boris S. Pushkarev and Jeffrey M. Zupan, *Public Transportation and Land Use Policy* (Indiana University Press, 1977), p. 39.

2. In 1980, 3.74 percent of all suburban-dwelling workers were employed in their central business districts in the twenty-five largest urban areas, and 3.33 percent in all cities. Data from Peter Gordon, Ajay Kumar, and Harry W.

Richardson, "Congestion, Changing Metropolitan Structure, and City Size in the United States," *International Regional Science Review*, vol. 12, no. 1 (1989), p. 49. In metropolitan areas containing 3 million or more residents, 15.4 percent of all workers used public transit for commuting in 1983, according to Federal Highway Administration, *Personal Travel in the U.S.*, vol. 1: *1983–1984 Nationwide Personal Transportation Study* (Department of Transportation, 1986), p. 7-12. But the same table showed that only 6.2 percent of such workers did so in all metropolitan areas. This covers only workers within metropolitan areas; in the entire nation, 4.6 percent of all workers commuted by public transportation in 1983.

Index